P9-DNO-272

7601 0100 527 453 3

IT HAPPENED TO ME

Series Editor: Arlene Hirschfelder

Books in the It Happened to Me series are designed for inquisitive teens digging for answers about certain illnesses, social issues, or lifestyle interests. Whether you are deep into your teen years or just entering them, these books are gold mines of up-to-date information, riveting teen views, and great visuals to help you figure out stuff. Besides special boxes highlighting singular facts, each book is enhanced with the latest reading lists, websites, and an index. Perfect for browsing, there are loads of expert information by acclaimed writers to help parents, guardians, and librarians understand teen illness, tough situations, and lifestyle choices.

1. *Epilepsy: The Ultimate Teen Guide,* by Kathlyn Gay and Sean McGarrahan, 2002.
2. *Stress Relief: The Ultimate Teen Guide,* by Mark Powell, 2002.
3. *Learning Disabilities: The Ultimate Teen Guide,* by Penny Hutchins Paquette and Cheryl Gerson Tuttle, 2003.
4. *Making Sexual Decisions: The Ultimate Teen Guide,* by L. Kris Gowen, 2003.
5. *Asthma: The Ultimate Teen Guide,* by Penny Hutchins Paquette, 2003.
6. *Cultural Diversity—Conflicts and Challenges: The Ultimate Teen Guide,* by Kathlyn Gay, 2003.
7. *Diabetes: The Ultimate Teen Guide,* by Katherine J. Moran, 2004.
8. *When Will I Stop Hurting? Teens, Loss, and Grief: The Ultimate Teen Guide to Dealing with Grief,* by Ed Myers, 2004.
9. *Volunteering: The Ultimate Teen Guide,* by Kathlyn Gay, 2004.
10. *Organ Transplants—A Survival Guide for the Entire Family: The Ultimate Teen Guide,* by Tina P. Schwartz, 2005.
11. *Medications: The Ultimate Teen Guide,* by Cheryl Gerson Tuttle, 2005.
12. *Image and Identity—Becoming the Person You Are: The Ultimate Teen Guide,* by L. Kris Gowen and Molly C. McKenna, 2005.
13. *Apprenticeship: The Ultimate Teen Guide,* by Penny Hutchins Paquette, 2005.
14. *Cystic Fibrosis: The Ultimate Teen Guide,* by Melanie Ann Apel, 2006.
15. *Religion and Spirituality in America: The Ultimate Teen Guide,* by Kathlyn Gay, 2006.

49. *Chronic Illnesses, Syndromes, and Rare Disorders: The Ultimate Teen Guide,* by Marlene Targ Brill, 2016.
50. *Autism Spectrum Disorder: The Ultimate Teen Guide,* by Francis Tabone, 2016.
51. *Sexual Assault: The Ultimate Teen Guide,* by Olivia Ghafoerkhan, 2016.

SEXUAL ASSAULT

THE ULTIMATE TEEN GUIDE

OLIVIA GHAFOERKHAN

IT HAPPENED TO ME, NO. 51

ROWMAN & LITTLEFIELD
Lanham • Boulder • New York • London

Published by Rowman & Littlefield
A wholly owned subsidiary of The Rowman & Littlefield Publishing Group, Inc.
4501 Forbes Boulevard, Suite 200, Lanham, Maryland 20706
www.rowman.com

Unit A, Whitacre Mews, 26-34 Stannary Street, London SE11 4AB

Copyright © 2017 by Rowman & Littlefield

All rights reserved. No part of this book may be reproduced in any form or by any electronic
or mechanical means, including information storage and retrieval systems, without written
permission from the publisher, except by a reviewer who may quote passages in a review.

British Library Cataloguing in Publication Information Available

Library of Congress Cataloging-in-Publication Data

Names: Ghafoerkhan, Olivia, 1982– author.
Title: Sexual assault : the ultimate teen guide / Olivia Ghafoerkhan.
Description: Lanham : Rowman & Littlefield, [2017] | Series: It happened to me ; No. 51 |
    Includes bibliographical references and index.
Identifiers: LCCN 2016020501 (print) | LCCN 2016031728 (ebook) | ISBN 9781442252479
    (hardback : alk. paper) | ISBN 9781442252486 (electronic)
Subjects: LCSH: Sex crimes—Juvenile literature. | Sexual abuse victims—Services for—Juvenile
    literature. | Sexually abused teenagers—Services for—Juvenile literature.
Classification: LCC HV6556 .G5165 2017 (print) | LCC HV6556 (ebook) | DDC
    362.8830835—dc23
LC record available at https://lccn.loc.gov/2016020501

∞™ The paper used in this publication meets the minimum requirements of American
National Standard for Information Sciences—Permanence of Paper for Printed Library
Materials, ANSI/NISO Z39.48-1992.

Printed in the United States of America

To the survivors of sexual assault,
to those who work to end sexual violence, and
to those who help survivors recover.
It is my hope that this book will add to the amazing work
being done by such individuals,
and that it will bring comfort and hope to survivors.

Contents

Acknowledgments

There are many people who contributed to making this book possible. I would like to thank Jodell Sadler, for putting me in contact with Rowman & Littlefield. A very special thanks goes to Arlene Hirschfelder, the series editor, for excellent feedback throughout this process. Thanks are due as well to Stephen Ryan, senior acquisitions editor; Andrea O. Kendrick, assistant editor; Jessica McCleary, assistant managing editor; and Jacqline Barnes, publicity and advertising. I greatly appreciate the help and support I've received from everyone at Rowman & Littlefield. Additionally, thanks to copy editor Gail Fay for her enthusiasm and support.

The Rape, Abuse and Incest National Network's Speakers Bureau and Pandora's Project were both kind enough to put me in touch with survivors who so generously shared their stories. Thank you to both of those organizations. Additionally, thanks go to Survivors Chat for permitting me to post about this work via Twitter and reach survivors that way. I also want to thank all those who shared and retweeted information about this book through social media, which spread the word to additional survivors.

Many individuals offered me support and guidance while I worked on this project. Sherry A. Falsetti, PhD, who specializes in post-traumatic stress disorder treatment, was kind enough to read the manuscript and check it for accuracy. Russell Grooms, one of the amazing librarians at the Woodbridge campus of Northern Virginia Community College, spent a morning helping me track down lost research. Julianna Baggott offered advice and generously answered some questions about publishing. Swati Avasthi gave valuable research suggestions. Judi Marcin offered much support for this project and introduced me to Sherry A. Falsetti. Additionally, I want to thank the Hamline MFA in Writing for Children and Young Adults program, all the wonderful writers who teach there, and my amazing class. That program was instrumental in helping me gain the skills needed to undertake a work of this complexity. Special thanks to Marquesas Blimes, Danielle Hale, Danielle Noyes, Tamara Simms, Rochelle Van Tassell, and Rebecca Watson, who have offered unwavering support and friendship throughout this process. Thanks are due as well to my children's babysitter, Hannah Griesmyer, and to the whole Griesmyer family for support during a stressful time.

I would be remiss to not thank my family for their love, support, and sacrifice. Thank you to my husband, Faiyaz, who provided emotional support and picked up more than his fair share of home and family duties to give me more time to write. Thank you to my children, who so graciously shared me with this book. Additionally, my in-laws stepped in to help when time, schedules, and deadlines became demanding. Thank you, Marcia and Nazreen, for lifting the burden for me when things got hard. And many thanks to my dad, my grandmother, and my sister, for all of their support.

There are many other individuals who, because of work or personal concerns, cannot be thanked by name. You know who you are and how much you're appreciated. There are also the many survivors, some of whom shared their stories and experiences and some who shared support for this work—thank you. Your support for this book means a great deal to me. I also feel it's only appropriate to thank my Heavenly Father for the added support and guidance and insight that I experienced while writing this book; my abilities were truly expanded to meet the demands of this task.

Introduction

This book represents over a year of intensive research and study. It also represents the stories and experiences of more than forty survivors of sexual assault. Not all of these stories made it into the book. Some survivors found the interview process or the writing process too difficult and needed to stop. Some survivors shared their stories, and then later decided that they were not ready for their stories to be made public. Many of them stayed in touch with me and remained very invested in this project.

In addition to the survivors who contacted me with the express intent to share their stories in this book, there were many other survivors who, although not ready to share publicly themselves, were incredibly supportive of this project. I was very public about this writing project on social media, in the classes I teach, at church, and with everyone I came in contact with. It surprised me in these daily interactions how many people with whom I'm personally acquainted have been the victims of sexual assault. As these individuals told me their stories, they also expressed their immense support and gratitude that this book was being written.

The survivors I spoke with, both on a personal level and in interviews for the book, were at all different places in their healing journey. Some were very much still hurting. Others were doing extremely well. The amount of time that had passed since the assaults varied and seemed to have very little relationship to how well the survivors were doing. From my observation, formal counseling and informal support from loved ones seemed to be the most important factors in a speedy recovery.

The other thing that surprised me was the number of people who approached me to share their knowledge on this topic in the form of rape myths, or false beliefs about rape. People said things like "You know women lie about being raped" and "Women should avoid dark parking lots because that's where a lot of rapes happen." Even when I explained the actual facts about sexual assault with these people—like the fact that sexual assault is falsely reported at roughly the same rate as other crimes and there's no evidence that women disproportionately falsely report, or that the majority of sexual assault victims are assaulted by someone they know—the individual presenting the false information would double down on his or her position. No amount of factual evidence to the contrary would persuade the person that what he or she believed about sexual assault was wrong.

After this happened several times, I came to the conclusion that people cling to these false ideas because it makes them feel better.

As a society, we don't want to admit the severity of the problem. We don't want to recognize that this is something that could happen to us or to someone we know. It makes us feel safe to imagine the rapist as a shadowy figure in a ski mask with a knife, lurking in dark alleys: that makes him easy to identify.

Several people sent me lists, handy tips to avoid being sexually assaulted— things like wear your hair loose. Hold your keys in your hand when walking to your car. Drive away as soon as you reach your car. Be careful where you park. Avoid white utility vans. And while I'm sure some of these have been factors in some assaults, none of them played a role in any of the stories I heard from survivors. In the forty-plus stories I heard, only four people were assaulted by strangers: two were assaulted by men who broke into their homes, one was abducted by carjacking, and one was mugged on the street and then assaulted. This proportion is consistent with statistics on sexual assault. The majority of assault victims whom I talked to were assaulted either by someone they were friends with, in a relationship with, or by a family member.

I've heard from many survivors who were met with silence when they told their families or loved ones what had happened to them. Their families didn't know what to say or how to offer support. So the sexual assault became an unspoken presence in the relationship. Many romantic relationships ended in the aftermath of an assault. I also spoke to many survivors who either blamed themselves or were blamed by their loved ones.

I think what is needed is more talk. Survivors need people to share their stories with; they need support. More than that, we need to have more conversations about what sexual assault and abuse look like. Yes, sometimes it is the guy in the ski mask. But sometimes it's a nice guy at church who wants to be a mentor. Sometimes it's a family friend. Sometimes it's a family member. Sometimes it's a sports coach or a teacher. Sometimes it's a coworker or even an employer. And sometimes it's the person you love. And it's never the victim's fault. Saying it's the victim's fault is saying that rape just happens. It is ignoring both the existence and the agency of the rapist who committed the crime. When a rape occurs, someone is making a choice and someone else is having his or her choice taken away.

It is my hope that this work will help dispel some of the common false beliefs about sexual assault. Chapter 7 focuses on some of these rape myths and provides factual information on those topics. I also hope this book will provide survivors of sexual assault with the resources and support they need to aid their recovery. Resources are provided throughout, and at the end there is a list of all the resources mentioned, including websites, nonfiction and fiction books, and films. In addition, chapter 9 is dedicated to the healing/recovery process and provides names of places where you can go for help. And because the rates of sexual assault are so high, it's very likely that all readers of this work will come in contact with someone who has been assaulted. Chapter 6 has a section to help friends know what to say if someone confides in them about an assault. It is my hope that this book will give you the tools you need to help and support a friend or loved one who has survived an assault.

WHAT IS SEXUAL ASSAULT?

When people hear the term *sexual assault* they often think of a man in a dark mask, hiding in an alley at night with a knife or a gun. People think of forcible rape by a stranger.

There are several different kinds of sexual assault, however. Rape is a form of sexual assault, but it's not the only one. Unwanted contact, such as kissing or groping, is also sexual assault. Any sexual contact without express consent is sexual assault.[1]

And that stranger waiting with a knife in the dark? In the majority of cases, about 82 percent, the perpetrator of the sexual assault is someone the victim knows.[2] And the weapon of choice for rapists? In 2001, only 11 percent of reported rapes involved the use of a weapon.[3]

Every year in the United States, there is an average of 293,066 victims of sexual assault and rape. That means that a sexual assault occurs roughly every 107 seconds. (This number of victims, however, does not include victims under the age of twelve.)[4] These are only the rapes that are reported in a year.

Statistics on sexual assault are gathered by researchers and psychologists using surveys and in-person interviews. Researchers use large population samples. Many of the statistics commonly used today have come from multiple studies. The majority of rapes go unreported to the police. Only 32 percent are actually reported. Because of the difficulty in gathering evidence and building a case in a majority of these cases, only about 7 percent of cases lead to an arrest. From there, only about 3 percent of cases go to trial, at which point 2 percent lead to an actual felony conviction. Out of a hundred rapes, only two rapists will spend a day in jail.[5]

One of the many factors contributing to the low rate of prosecution and felony conviction is the nation's backlog of untested rape kits. Rape kits are administered in hospitals and are used to collect the physical DNA evidence that is left behind after a sexual assault. DNA evidence has been instrumental in both convicting the guilty and freeing those wrongfully imprisoned. Unfortunately, the majority of these rape kits will be housed in storage facilities and evidence

> ### *Something Happened* by Greg Logsted
>
> The main character in this young adult novel, Billy, is still grieving the loss of his father when he is befriended by his eighth grade English teacher. At first the interactions are innocent, but the teacher quickly turns from a concerned bystander to a predator as the work progresses. The sexual assault in this book is kissing, with an attempt at something more, but at Billy's young age this interaction with a teacher is very damaging. This book illustrates the confusion and harm that sexual assault from an authority figure can cause someone.[a]

rooms, gathering dust for decades. This problem is often referred to as the rape kit backlog. While it's hard to know for sure exactly how many rape kits are currently sitting untested, the US Department of Justice estimates the number to be as high as four hundred thousand.[6]

The following story from Destiny, a survivor of sexual assault, illustrates how perpetrators will groom a victim, working to gain her trust before using that same trust to sexually exploit her. In this story, the grooming process took place over several months:

> When I was nineteen, a church member harassed and sexually assaulted me for months. I'll call him "Roy." Roy and I had attended the same church for years, but we didn't know each other well. I spent most of my time with other teens in the church youth group. He was a few years older than me. (Found out he was in his late thirties after the assaults!) But one day, Roy asked if we could get to know each other better. At first I said no since I didn't know him. So his aunt assured me he was simply a gentleman that "mentored" young women in the church. But he wasn't a mentor at all; he was a predator.
>
> Over the next four months, Roy called every now and then to see how I was doing and invited me out to eat when I wanted to talk about school. But something was off. When I'd see him in public or stop by his house with his aunt, he was kind and kept to himself. But he morphed into a monster once I saw him alone. He mixed alcohol in my drinks without telling me, made sly comments about my body, slipped his hands under my clothes and joked about having his way with me. Plus his aunt would

mention Roy thought I was *special* and had been watching me for years. That didn't sound right, but I felt trapped! Any time I tried to stay away, Roy threatened to ruin my reputation at church. He said it was my fault he acted the way he did behind closed doors. Out of fear, I'd go back to his house. I was stuck in his sick game and didn't know how to escape. With each visit, his aggression spiked. Fondling and joking escalated to pinning me down, wrapping his hands around my neck and raping me. . . . Afterwards, Roy would ridicule me, calling me names like slut, damaged goods, and tease. Then he'd brag about having a shady past no one knew about.

At the time this occurred, I believed the abuse was my fault. And I was overwhelmed. At church, Roy was this upstanding guy people looked up to every Sunday. So who'd believe me if I accused him of sexual assault? Roy used that to his advantage to keep me quiet until I got away. Looking back, there were a lot of red flags he wasn't a good guy. But I believed Roy's cruel lies. Honestly, I don't think that was the first time Roy and his aunt pulled their "mentor" scam. I believe they had a pattern of preying on young women at church.

I felt so broken and dirty after everything Roy had done to me. I loved my church family, but thinking of them reminded me of the abuse. I couldn't handle that, so I left church. And I questioned my faith in God. Why did this happen? Why me? I didn't tell anyone what happened until I broke down two years later. The pain I'd hidden felt like an infected wound, slowly oozing through my scars, leaking into every area of my life. The more I held on to the secret, the more I broke down. When I hit my breaking point, I reached out to a professor and told her what had occurred. She believed me and told me to get help. Soon, I was referred to counseling services at my university.[7]

The Victims

Anyone can be a victim of sexual assault. The majority of victims are female; about one out of every six US women are victims of rape or attempted rape. However, about 3 percent, or one in every thirty-three men, are victims too. And 15 percent of sexual assault victims are children under the age of twelve.[8]

Challenges Faced by Victims of Color

Victims of color face additional challenges. The reporting rates are much lower, even though assault rates are roughly similar for most groups, with the exception of Native American/Alaska Native women, for whom assault rates are higher.

What Is Consent, and Who Can Give It?

Sexual assault is a sexual act that the victim has not consented to. Consent is saying yes. An absence of a *no* does not mean consent. It's important to communicate clearly and ask questions in any sexual encounter to ensure that the situation is consensual. However, there are certain situations in which a person cannot legally give consent for sex. These situations include

- having a mental handicap,
- being intoxicated (on drugs or alcohol),
- being unconscious, and
- being underage.

The age at which an individual can give consent to engage in sexual activities varies from state to state. Some states, like Hawaii, Indiana, and the District of Columbia, set the age of consent at sixteen. Other states set it at seventeen or eighteen. States may also have special laws that make it legal to give consent if the two people are close in age; for example, in the District of Columbia. Even though the age of consent there is sixteen, there is an exception for cases where the two people are only four years or less apart in age; for instance, it would be legal for a fifteen-year-old to have sex with an eighteen-year-old. These types of laws have been termed Romeo and Juliet laws.[b] If there are no legal exceptions like a Romeo and Juliet law, then if the person is under the age of consent, even if she or he agrees to a sexual act, it is legally considered statutory rape.[c]

Each ethnic group faces its own unique challenges that are impacted by historical oppression, but there are some common problems they all face. One is institutional racism. Women of color are less likely to be treated with respect and are less likely to be believed when reporting a sexual assault at a police station or hospital. They face similar challenges when seeking counseling or other services; they could face similar racial stereotypes or have to work with staff or counselors who are not trained or educated about the concerns that people of color face. Women of color are also often overly sexualized in the media, creating stereotypes that any assault experienced by these women isn't "real rape."[9]

For African American women, the reporting rates are especially low. It's estimated that for every African American woman who reports a rape, there are at least fifteen who do not report. Black women are less likely to be believed when reporting a rape because of stereotypes in movies and other media that have painted them as being overly sexual. These myths minimize the harm done in a sexual assault and make pursuing justice more difficult.[10]

A little less than 7 percent of Asian and Pacific Islander individuals are found to report rape. This low reporting rate is attributed to cultural values of keeping victimization private. Asian and Pacific Islander women also face racial stereotypes as being "submissive" and "sexually available," causing them to often be the victims of sexual harassment, sometimes from people in authority who should be available to help them.[11]

While Hispanic and Latina women are sexually assaulted at a similar rate as women of other races, they are more likely to disclose being raped by a partner at some point in their lifetime. Because of cultural beliefs, such as the belief that sex is a marital obligation, Hispanic and Latina women may take longer to identify an assault from a partner as rape. Hispanic and Latina women face challenges in reporting sexual assault as well. Stereotypes that they all speak the same language or that they are in the United States illegally can greatly impact how they experience the reporting process with the police and with other assistance and services they may try to utilize. Cultural stereotypes, such as the view that a woman who is raped is promiscuous, may prevent her from reporting and seeking help.[12]

Native American and Alaska Native women are three and a half times more likely to be raped than women from all other races. About one in three, or a little over 34 percent, of Native women are victims of rape. And in about nine out of ten of those rape cases, the assailant is white or black. To make this situation more difficult, the jurisdiction for Native people is more complicated. For a long time, Indian nations did not have the authority to prosecute non-Native offenders. This left Native people, especially Native women, extremely vulnerable to abuse. And while the US Department of Justice has jurisdiction to prosecute felonies committed against Native people, these crimes are rarely prosecuted. Native people are also limited in their ability to seek outside help and services due to racial and oppressive practices that are both historical and personal for native people.[13] When the Violence Against Women Act was reauthorized in 2013, it contained a special provision to address these issues. This provision, granting Indian nations "special domestic violence criminal jurisdiction," allows tribal courts to prosecute cases of domestic violence, dating violence, and sexual assault, regardless of whether the perpetrator is Native or non-Native. This new provision is a huge step toward ensuring safety for Native women.[14]

There is less known, and less available, research about the experiences of men of color who have been the victims of sexual assault. This is in part because of societal trends and stereotypes that criminalize minority men or build them up as being ultra-masculine. Because of these images of what a black man or what a Latino man is supposed to be or look like, these groups are generally not willing to participate in studies attempting to gather data about their experiences. Several famous African American men have spoken publicly about their experiences with childhood sexual abuse, men such as R&B performer R. Kelly, CNN anchor Don Lemon, and actor/producer/writer Tyler Perry.[15]

Another marginalized group that experiences problems reporting sexual assault and accessing services are those who identify as LGBTQ (lesbian, gay, bisexual, transgender, queer/questioning). Sexual assault rates for LGBTQ individuals are similar, or higher, than those of heterosexual individuals. In the case of transgender individuals, however, that rate is much higher: 64 percent of transgender individuals are victims of sexual assault.[16]

In some cases, sexual assaults of LGBTQ individuals, or individuals perceived to be LGBTQ, are hate crimes by people who are homophobic or transphobic. In other cases, sexual assault can come from intimate partners or from within the LGBTQ community. In either case, seeking help and services can be difficult. LGBTQ individuals may be reluctant to identify when reporting to police or other services because of homophobia and transphobia, making it difficult to get access to services that are geared toward LGBTQ individuals.[17] When the sexual assault comes from within the LGBTQ community, there may be a reluctance to report or seek help because of loyalty to the community and fear of reinforcing negative stereotypes about LGBTQ people.[18]

Among LGBTQ individuals, those who also identify as people of color are at an even greater risk of being sexually assaulted. There is the possibility that racism and homophobia combine to put these individuals at a greater disadvantage. When these individuals seek help, they have the compounded challenges of reporting as a person of color and as a LGBTQ person.[19]

The following story is from Jannina, a twenty-three-year-old survivor who was victimized twice. She was the victim of childhood sexual assault and of date rape/acquaintance rape. Although she does not draw the conclusion herself, it appears that both her boss and her coworker intentionally got her intoxicated in order to facilitate the rape:

It was the fourth day of work. I had just turned eighteen. We were having a lifeguard staff meeting and all of my coworkers were there. After the meeting I had two hours for lunch and had planned on just staying at the

Sexual assault can be confusing for young men because of stereotypes about masculinity.

pool and resting. I didn't have any money and hadn't brought any food so I was planning on waiting until I got home later that night to eat. My boss came up to me after the meeting and asked me what I was doing for lunch. I told her nothing and she asked if I wanted to go with her to a bar where she was going to grab some lunch. I told her I wasn't twenty-one yet and that I didn't really have any money. She responded saying it wasn't a big deal and that she knew a woman who worked there who wouldn't card me and that she would pay for lunch. I was so excited. I really wanted to seem cool and make a good impression on her. Another coworker said he'd come with us and so the three of us took off. It was about ten blocks away and a couple of avenues over and so we decided to walk there. When we arrived, they ordered a round of margaritas. Now, my parents had been very strict growing up. I had never drank before in my life and was really excited and confident that I'd be fine. However, I remember my father's voice once warning me that if I ever drank, to never do so on an empty stomach. There were some chips and salsa on the table, so I began to eat those in hopes they'd do something to fill my empty stomach. They didn't do much. I really liked the margarita and drank it a lot more quickly than I had planned to. My face got flushed and I waited patiently and silently for whatever they were planning on ordering for food. They replaced the chips and salsa with more and ordered another round. I began to feel funny and light headed. I tried to eat more chips but that made it worse, so after finishing the second margarita, I excused myself to the bathroom, thanking them, and telling them I'd had enough. It became clear they weren't going to order anything to eat, and I had to be back at work soon. When I got back to the table, to my surprise and horror, they had ordered me another margarita. I was really not feeling well, but not wanting to seem uncool, I began to drink the third one. I began to feel really sick so after I had finished, I excused myself and headed back to work. The once short walk seemed endless on the way back and I stumbled my way back to the pool. I was having double vision and felt horrible. I was so drunk, and had no idea what to do.

When I got there, I opened the pool and thankfully, there were no swimmers. I sat there trying to steady myself and just prayed over and over again that God would take the feeling away. Thirty minutes later my coworker showed up with a six pack of beer. I asked him what he was doing there and he said he figured I could use some company. Too drunk to care I said okay and he pulled up a seat next to me and opened me up a bottle. I took a sip and it was like the world gave way underneath me. I felt like I had to throw up and told him I was going to be sick. He said not to worry, that he knew what that was, and that I should jump into the pool because the water would make me feel better. I hadn't been issued a bathing suit yet so he told me he had an extra pair of swim trunks and that I could just wear those and the t-shirt and I'd be fine. I clumsily changed into those and jumped in the pool. The water felt nice and kinda made me feel a little bit better. But he jumped in with me. He began to swim near me and I tried to swim discretely away each time. The movement started making my stomach feel worse and I couldn't hold it in anymore and I told him to watch the pool for me while I went to the bathroom. He said sure, but that I had to use the men's bathroom because the woman's was out of order. Again, too sick to care, I rushed to the men's bathroom. I didn't make it to the stall, I made it into the shower area where I began to vomit all over the place. It felt like my body was letting out my insides and I turned the shower on to wash it away as I just kept on throwing up. The water was loud. I didn't hear him come in. I didn't think this would ever happen to me. I didn't see the signs. Next thing I know I feel his hands grab my waist from behind me and in a split second, he lowered my shorts and in that moment he took me. He used me, he defiled me. For hours he had his way with me, forced himself into every part of me and I was too weak to fight back. Too weak to even scream as I kept vomiting and crying through it all. A resident would eventually come in and see four feet in the bathroom stall and call in to say he needed the pool. The coworker rushed out, leaving me on the shower floor, covered in vomit and filth. I cleaned up the best I could and walked out and back on the pool deck. He had left and I reopened the pool for the resident and got back on duty. Fifteen minutes later I got a call from my boss. She told me a resident had called to complain that there was a woman in the men's bathroom and that the pool had been closed. She wanted to know what had happened because my coworker had called her claiming he'd "bagged the new girl." She asked me for the truth and so I saw my way out. I would make my own truth. I told her nothing had happened, I told her that the co-worker wished he'd bagged me and that the resident was crazy because I'd been there the whole time. She believed me, and that became the truth. He came back the next day to talk about his victory and asked me if I'd liked it, I told him I didn't know what he was talking about. He quit a week later and I never saw him again. I told no one. For three years, no one knew.[20]

Kinds of Sexual Assault

There are many different kinds of sexual assault and groups that are affected by sexual assault. In the following chapters, some of these kinds of assault will be looked at in depth, but here is some basic information on many of the different kinds of sexual violence.

Stranger Assault

This is what people most commonly think of when they think of sexual assault. In reality, four out of five victims know their assailant. There are different categories of stranger assault: Blitz sexual assault is when a stranger attacks an individual quickly, usually at night in a public place. This is the stranger lurking in the alley. Home invasion sexual assault is when the perpetrator breaks into a home and then assaults the victim. Contact sexual assault is when the perpetrator flirts with the victim or otherwise lures or coerces the victim to a place so the assault can occur.[21]

Childhood Sexual Assault or Child Sexual Abuse

As many as 93 percent of victims of child sexual abuse know the perpetrator. It can be a family member, a family friend, or anyone else the child has contact with. Child sexual abuse includes child pornography, an adult exposing him- or herself to a child, masturbation, fondling, and any kind of sexual intercourse. Child sexual abuse is especially damaging because it is a violation of trust during early developmental years.[22]

Date Rape or Acquaintance Rape

This type of assault happens when the perpetrator has developed a relationship with the victim, then pressures or forces the victim into sexual acts. Drugs and alcohol may or may not be used to facilitate the assault. For many years this kind of rape wasn't identified as a crime. Today there still needs to be increased awareness about this kind of rape. Because friendship precedes the assault, the victim may be confused or may blame him- or herself for the assault.[23]

Campus Assault

Young women in college are especially vulnerable to date rape or acquaintance rape. More than 90 percent of sexual assaults on college campuses go unreported. Recently, legislation and the media have begun to confront this issue, pushing for changes in how college campuses handle sexual assault.[24]

Intimate Partner Sexual Violence

Sexual assault can occur in intimate relationships too, both in dating and in marriage. In these relationships, sexual assault rarely occurs without other types of abuse occurring as well.[25] Recent studies have examined the prevalence of teen dating violence, which includes sexual assault as well as other kinds of abuse.[26]

Military Sexual Assault or Military Sexual Trauma

Based on a recent study, roughly 1 percent of servicemen and close to 5 percent of servicewomen were sexually assaulted in 2014. This equates to about 10,600 men

A Dangerous Crossroads:
Sexual Assault on Military Campuses

While there has been increased focus on sexual assault on college campuses, and on sexual assaults within the armed forces, there is one place where this issue is being neglected: our military academies.

About 8 percent of cadets and midshipmen at the academies of the armed forces were sexually assaulted in 2014. Only about half of those assaults were reported. Close to half of cadets and midshipmen experienced sexual harassment.

Reports of sexual assault and sexual harassment at the academies follow a chain of command within the academy. There can be an appeal, but it follows the same chain of command.

The situation is escalated by what can be termed a sexist environment within the academies themselves. For example, it's been reported that sexist chants are taught to cadets, who are then required to sing them when marching: "I wish that all the ladies were holes in the road and I was a dump truck. I'd fill 'em with my load."[d]

And unlike college victims of sexual assault, cadets and midshipmen at the academies do not qualify for Title IX protection that allows for reporting the mishandling of sexual assault cases to the Department of Education. There is no recourse outside of the academy to which victims can turn.[e]

and 9,600 women. Men were more likely to be assaulted by multiple perpetrators in a single incident and were less likely to report the assault. In assaults involving women, alcohol was more likely to be involved. This is another area of sexual violence that has been gaining more attention recently.[27]

Human Trafficking and Sexual Exploitation

Human trafficking, and especially sex trafficking, is a global problem and is a major issue in the United States. Traffickers prey on runaway teens and other vulnerable

Efforts to Address Sexual Slavery in the United States

In 2013, the FBI coordinated a nationwide sweep of seventy-six cities. The sweep took place over three days, resulting in 150 arrests and the recovery of 105 children. The children, who ranged in age from thirteen to seventeen years old, were all being used for commercial sexual activities. They were being solicited on the Internet, on street corners, at truck stops, and in casinos. The sweep, titled Operation Cross Country, is part of a national campaign that launched in 2005. Treating underage prostitutes as victims rather than criminals is a step in the right direction.[f]

youth, such as minorities and LGBTQ teens, as well as teens from abusive homes. Usually a trafficker will establish a romantic relationship with the victim, convince the victim to run away or leave his or her current situation, and then force the victim into commercial sexual acts. The National Center for Missing and Exploited Children estimated that one in six runaways reported to the center in 2014 were victims of human trafficking.[28]

Prisoner Rape

This refers to any unwanted sexual contact experienced by a prison inmate. The unwanted contact could come from another prisoner or from prison guards and other staff members. In 2003 the Prison Rape Elimination Act was passed in order to facilitate research into the problem of prisoner rape, and as a means of providing victims of prisoner rape with better resources and services.[29]

The Psychological Damage from Sexual Assault

The following story, which originally appeared in *Salon* in April of 2015, shows some of the psychological damage from sexual assault. Laura's story is unique because the perpetrator was caught and prosecuted:

Is It Enough?

Is the Prison Rape Elimination Act doing enough to address sexual assault within the prison system? After the passing of the act in 2003, it took nine years for guidelines to be issued to states. But the cost of not complying with the guidelines is relatively minor: states that don't comply may lose 5 percent of the federal funds they receive for prisons. As of now, only two states are in compliance, forty-one are trying to get there, and seven have chosen not to follow the guidelines at all.

But for the prisoners, there's the question of whom to report sexual assault to when about half of the sexual assaults in prisons are committed by prison personnel.

Societal acceptance of prison rape is alarmingly high, with prison rape jokes being common. Some even view rape as part of the punishment. However, the Constitution protects citizens from cruel and unusual punishment, and prisoners, as well as their health and well-being, are the responsibility of the state.[9]

I tried to explain it to someone once. It's like surviving your own murder, sort of. Ever wonder who would show up at your funeral? Or, more to the point: Who would actually be sad? . . .

By two o'clock in the afternoon I will be in the hospital, nurses and social workers reciting health risks and injecting me with things and swabbing and scraping the "evidence" off my body. Later, I will be billed for this: over a thousand for the kit, a few hundred for the ambulance, two hundred or so for the doctor who finally appeared after I sat, waiting, glassy-eyed with ringing ears, for some hours. But for all the hours that pass, the handprints are still around my neck, a broken circle of red and gray.

My boyfriend will find me there, and I will hear for the first time from a boy the three-word phrase most girls imagine hearing on a romantic evening out, arms entwined, leaned in to each other against the backdrop of a city skyline or a beach. But we are in a private waiting room at a hospital with harsh fluorescent lighting, hard plastic folding chairs and an audience of two social workers and a cop, when in between gasps of dry sobbing (no tears yet, too much going on for tears, tears will come later) come the words: I love you.

It is true, what the song says—it's a cold and it's a broken hallelujah. In a few years' time, we will part ways. It is a slower process for him than for me, but he, too, will be drained of everything he was before the afternoon of November 11, will become someone else entirely, and the life we built together will dry up and crumble under the pressure of what I am told is called "survival."

My roommate arrives and he tells me a phrase many friends parrot over the course of the next few weeks: You don't have to talk about anything. At first, this is fine, I don't necessarily want to talk about "anything," especially since I have to talk about "anything" ad nauseam with detectives and the district attorney. But it is only a short time before I learn that "you don't have to talk about it" means "I don't want to hear about it." One of my oldest friends is so committed to not hearing about it that three years pass before we speak again at all. Every time, "you don't have to talk about it," rather than "I want to hear about it." How many doors we can close with the nuances of language. Personal tragedies create their own bystander effect.

I leave the hospital with pamphlets and numbers and paperwork that I abandon in the back of a squad car. I have nothing else, no wallet or even keys, having been escorted out of my apartment so quickly by the police when they finally came—or, rather, when I finally opened the door, too afraid to open it at first, afraid he might still be there, might be hiding, might have the gun out, and then when I did finally open the door, I ran for it, throwing it open and dropping to my knees in front of an exasperated female officer, clinging to her feet, wanting only to be wrapped in the maternal safety she represented while someone other than me said help me, help me, please God, help me, please, please, underneath shouts of what did he look like? and which way did he go? and what do you mean this isn't what you were wearing? before they realized it wasn't just a robbery. Call SVU, we need SVU on the scene, get a bus.

Outside of the hospital, it is dark outside, nighttime—the actual hour, I have no idea, one's concept of time evaporates in the back of a police car—when the detectives take us from the hospital and steer us through Harlem. While driving up Amsterdam back to my apartment we behold a completely ludicrous sight passing us in the opposite lane: an enormous flatbed truck, headed downtown towing the Rockefeller Center Christmas tree. Someone might have commented on it (as it was grotesquely hilarious given the circumstances), but I was fighting nausea from antibiotics and antiretrovirals and, in such disbelief that I was even alive, confused by the fact that Christmas would still be happening, that the rest of the world was preparing for the holiday season when it would be three years before I gave much thought to any date other than November 11. I say nothing, but I watch it pass, try to turn around and follow it through the rear window, but am stopped by so many aches: my left arm, from the injections; my neck and jaw, from someone else's hands. . . .

As we slow to a stop on 147th, now uselessly decorated in yellow tape from Broadway to Amsterdam, the investigation reveals more pieces of my life that have been strewn about for public display—literally. The detectives believe they have found the dress I had been wearing earlier that day dumped in the trash on a corner. I am asked to identify it. Navy blue, brass buttons, pockets. It is indeed the dress, the one I had immediately fallen in love with at first glance and purchased only the day before. Remember when I said the tears would come—later? Later is now.

I am called upon to watch a surveillance video at a bodega and then give the detectives a walk-through of my apartment, to further illustrate the story I'd told at least a dozen times that day in painstaking graphic detail. I am accompanied by what seems to me like an absurd amount of police officers. One of them asks about the pills they gave me at the hospital, tells me I should eat something to settle my stomach before they kick in. I am struck by the kindness of it, given that neither the nurse nor the HIV counselor recommended the same.

People seem to think Olivia Benson is real, that there's a benevolent maternal figure to escort you through criminal proceedings with a hand that is both comforting and knowledgeable. But she isn't real, although *Law & Order: SVU* would make an episode loosely based on my case one year later. My mother was horrified that I wasn't "provided with" a female detective, as if these are decisions that can be made as though one is choosing between two different dress colors. But there is comfort to be found in strange, peripheral places: the officer who suggested food, the security guard at the courthouse who would embrace me after the lead detective on my case whispered something in her ear, the bailiff at my trial three years later who made sure I was comfortable while I sat alone in the witness-holding room, the presiding judge who would also hug and congratulate me as though I'd just walked the stage at my graduation. The assistant district attorney handling my case was wonderful and brilliant and more of a practical help to me than any of the social workers and counselors I was sent to see, one of whom dumbly informed me through a fluorescent smile that I should consider getting a dog. My friends and family, for the most part, kept a distance, the formal length of an arm, broaching the topic with polite rarity. I get it. You can't hug someone closely and watch them at the same time. . . .

This is the most insidious sensation and the most haunting, as it will call every relationship you have into question. You will try to convince yourself it's not true, that only a small evil subset of the human population would ever do something so vicious. But your mail carrier, your boss, your grandmother—no one will look the same. Even your own reflection will force you to consider what glitch could turn your brain into harsh gray lines of static. This is what the people around me didn't want to know, didn't want to hear, didn't want to see. *You don't have to talk about it. Please don't tell me about it.* To have lived through interpersonal violence is to have seen a glimpse of what the end of the world will look like and then asked to describe it, and in so doing, you must try to shield those you love from the reality of it by saying *it's not so bad, we're all going to be OK,* ushering them away from the edge, all the while looking over your shoulder to make sure you aren't being followed.

And then, when it's over, the funeral. Like at all funerals, there are the handful of true broken hearts—the family, the best friend, the boyfriend. Then there are those who come to pay their respects, politely, offering flowers, maybe a dinner, before going back to their daily routines while pushing to the back of their minds the idea that maybe something has been permanently altered. But then there are those who choose to not show at all, dizzy from the mere thought of looking over the edge, who would rather never speak of it at all and hold onto the idea of you they had before November 11. Can you blame them? Who would want to know the truth when it's so easy to ignore? Maybe they are the ones who know better, who can hold on to the hope that they will never have to see up close, in high definition, what so many people have been forced to see. I am saddened by their absence, but I hope they don't either.[30]

Sexual assault can cause long lasting psychological harm to the victim. It can cause post-traumatic stress disorder (PTSD), depression, eating disorders, substance abuse, and suicidal thoughts and self-harm. Flashbacks, which are a symptom of PTSD, are also common. There is also the risk of other health problems, like sexually transmitted diseases and the possibility of pregnancy.[31]

Victims of sexual assault can face additional challenges when sharing their assault with others. Because of the image people have of the masked stranger with a weapon hiding at night, they may not view other rape narratives as "real" rape. There is a tendency to blame the victim if she was dressed a certain way, if she drank alcohol, or if she didn't resist the assault. Some even have a belief that when a woman says no she really means yes and that women enjoy being sexually assaulted.[32] These rape myths aren't just emotionally harmful; they can prevent assault victims from getting the help they need.

If You Experience a Sexual Assault

Everyone experiences the trauma of sexual assault differently. It's important to know that regardless of the circumstances of the sexual assault, it is not your fault. No matter what choices you made prior to the assault, it is the perpetrator who made the decision to commit a crime.

There are many options available to you to report or seek help after an assault, but you do not have to report the assault.

A good first place to go for help and support is your local rape crisis center. Most rape crisis centers have advocates who can go with you to the hospital or the police station should you decide to report the assault. Crisis centers often offer free or low-cost counseling for victims of sexual assault. If you prefer to speak to someone anonymously, the Rape, Abuse and Incest National Network (RAINN) hotline is another option. You can call the hotline at 1-800-656-4673. A trained staff member will help put you in touch with local resources. There is also RAINN's online chat at ohl.rainn.org/online/. RAINN's website also has a link that allows you to look up your local rape crisis center.[33]

Depending on the severity of the assault, you may need medical attention. Even if you don't, going to your local hospital is a good idea. At the hospital trained nurses can administer a rape kit to collect DNA evidence from the assault. It's important not to wash prior to going to the hospital. Even if you delay going,

Fault Line by Christa Desir

Fault Line looks at both victim blaming and secondary trauma. The story is told from the point of view of Ben, who does not attend a party with his girlfriend, Ani. At the party Ani is gang-raped. The novel examines the tendency in the aftermath of a rape to find someone to blame. Was it Ben's fault for not going to the party with Ani? Was it Ani's friend Kate's fault for not intervening at the party? Was it Ani's fault for drinking? The work also looks closely at Ben's reaction and struggles to deal with Ani's rape, and his inability to help her afterward.[h]

DNA evidence can be collected up to seventy-two hours after an assault has taken place. You don't have to report the assault to the police in order to have a rape kit administered; the hospital will store the rape kit until you are ready to report the assault to the police.[34] The amount of time that a rape kit will be stored by the hospital varies from state to state, so you will want to ask the nurse performing the exam how long the kit will be stored. It's important to keep in mind that the amount of time a kit can be stored may not match up with the time limit for taking legal action. If you are considering pressing charges after an assault, you need to find out the statute of limitations for legal action in your state.[35]

When recovering from a sexual assault, it is important to care for yourself both physically and emotionally. Eat well, sleep well, and exercise. Journaling can be very therapeutic. Seek counseling. Remember that not all counselors are trained to work with sexual assault victims, so it's a good idea to ask. You can also seek support from your local rape crisis center or from a multitude of online support groups.[36]

Often survivors have to act fine and continue with their daily life in spite of the trauma they have experienced. They often suppress feelings related to the assault.

This chapter is just a brief overview of types of sexual assault, the harm caused by sexual assault, and the reporting process. All of these topics will be covered in more depth in the following chapters, which also provide additional resources for survivors of sexual assault.

Federal Laws and Legislation Regarding Sexual Assault

As awareness is raised about sexual assault and different forms of sexual violence, laws and legislation are passed to try to meet the needs of victims. Some of these laws, like the Violence Against Women Act, have been around since 1994 and are regularly reauthorized by Congress.

Even though there are laws in place, it's important that legislation continues to match growing knowledge of sexual assault and the needs of victims.

Here are some of the current federal laws relevant to sexual assault, in order by year:

- **1972:** Patsy T. Mink Equal Opportunity in Education Act (Title IX). Originally passed to prevent discrimination in schools on the basis of gender, Title IX has since been interpreted as a requirement for schools to protect students from sexual harassment and sexual assault. This law applies to colleges and universities that receive federal funding, including those that receive student financial aid. Colleges are required to protect students from gender crimes, including sexual assault. Victims must be provided with safety and support, and cannot be retaliated against for reporting Title IX violations. Title IX also requires colleges to have established procedures for addressing sexual assault complaints and other sex-based discrimination. Students can hold colleges legally responsible for failing to keep them safe.[37]
- **1984:** Victims of Crime Act (VOCA). This bill is designed to assist victims in handling the costs incurred by a crime. For victims of sexual assault, this could include the costs associated with medical care, time missed from work, or counseling/mental health expenses. The Crime Victim's Fund established by the VOCA also provides grants to agencies and programs that provide services to victims. The fund is supported by convicted criminals, through fines that they are required to pay as part of sentencing.[38]
- **1990:** Jeanne Clery Disclosure of Campus Security Policy and Campus Crime Statistics (Clery) Act. In 1986 a college freshmen named Jeanne Clery was raped and murdered in her on-campus residence. This event raised awareness about unreported crimes on college campuses. In response Congress passed the Clery Act. The Clery Act has been amended five times, most recently in 2013 with the passing of the Campus SaVE

Act. The Clery Act required campuses to keep records of certain crimes, including sexual crimes, occurring on or near campus, and to issue an annual report. The identities of victims are protected under the Clery Act. It also requires colleges to notify students of any ongoing security risks on campus.[39]

- **1994:** Violence Against Women Act (VAWA). The VAWA was the first federal legislation that recognized domestic violence, including sexual assault, as crimes. It provided federal funding to combat domestic violence. Each reauthorization of the VAWA has further strengthened it.

- **2003:** Prison Rape Elimination Act (PREA). The PREA was passed in order to both gather information about sexual assault crimes in prisons and offer support services to inmates who are victims of sexual assault. Prisoners are provided access to cost-free rape kits, sexual assault service providers, and support services.[40]

- **2004:** Debbie Smith Act. A stranger broke into Debbie Smith's home in 1989 and sexually assaulted her. A rape kit was performed, and although DNA evidence was collected, it went unanalyzed for over five years. When, in 1994, the forensic evidence was finally entered into the Combined DNA Index System (CODIS), which is the FBI's national database, the perpetrator was identified. He was already incarcerated and serving 161 years for the abduction of two women. He was brought to trial and convicted for raping Debbie Smith. The purpose of the Debbie Smith Act is to begin addressing the nation's backlog of untested rape kits. It was originally passed in 2004 and has been reauthorized twice. The act provides funding for crime labs to test rape kits and process the DNA evidence. It also requires states to create a plan to address the rape kit backlog. By increasing the amount of DNA evidence that is being processed, the Debbie Smith Act is helping to strengthen the CODIS, which in turn helps to bring more rapists to justice.[41]

- **2013:** Campus Sexual Violence Elimination (Campus SaVE) Act. The Campus SaVE Act was passed to amend the Clery Act of 1990. Campus SaVE provides college campuses with additional guidelines for how to handle sexual assault. Colleges are required to provide victims with a list of services available, both on and off campus, such as counseling, legal assistance, mental and health care, and victim advocacy. Additionally, colleges have to provide education and awareness programs to help prevent sexual assault and encourage bystander intervention. Colleges are also required to provide increased information in their annual security reports.[42]

- **2013:** Sexual Assault Forensic Evidence Reporting (SAFER) Act. The SAFER Act was passed to assist in efforts to address the nation's backlog of rape kits. It increases funding to process DNA evidence and provides

Tapestries of Hope: A Documentary of Zimbabwe

Sexual assault is a global problem. In 2007, director Michealene Cristini Risley travelled to Zimbabwe. There she met with human rights activist Betty Makoni, the founder of the Girl Child Network. Risley interviewed Betty and several survivors of rape in Zimbabwe. Through the filming and the interviewing process, Risley uncovered several startling myths, like the belief that a man can be cured of HIV/AIDS if he rapes a virgin. The documentary also explores the healing process of these survivors. During filming, Risley and her assistant were arrested and incarcerated. The Zimbabwean Intelligence Office also seized the film. Fortunately, Risley was able to retrieve the footage before being deported. *Tapestries of Hope* was released in 2011, and runs one hour and eighteen minutes.[i]

---

grants to help in the auditing and processing of rape kits stored in crime labs.[43]

- **2013:** Violence Against Women Reauthorization Act of 2013. The latest reauthorization of the Violence Against Women Act brought significant changes. It expanded the law to protect more individuals who are vulnerable to domestic violence, including LGBT victims, Native women, immigrants, college students, and teens. It now includes dating violence and stalking as well as all other forms of domestic violence.[44]

In addition to these federal laws, each state has its own laws related to sexual assault. You can look up the laws for your state on an online database on the RAINN website at www.rainn.org/public-policy.[45]

Even with existing laws and legislation, there is still more that can be done to improve the way the nation, states, and college campuses respond to and handle sexual assault. The final chapter of this book will look at different ways individuals can make a difference in improving how sexual assault is perceived, how victims are treated, and what services and legal resources are available to them.

DATE RAPE AND SEXUAL ASSAULT ON CAMPUSES

High school and college years are often spent in a whirl of social activities. Large parties with alcohol are common. Unfortunately, sexual predators see these types of gatherings as opportunities to prey on people who may have had a little too much to drink or who may have taken drugs.

Currently, it's estimated that one in five women will be sexually assaulted during college,[1] and that one in sixteen men will be as well.[2] These statistics come from anonymous surveys. It's hard to get accurate numbers by other means because only about 32 percent of rapes are reported to the police.[3]

What Are Date Rape Drugs?

There are several kinds of date rape drugs that can be slipped into drinks. They include rohypnol, GHB, and ketamine. These drugs can cause blurred vision and memory loss, and they can have a paralyzing effect.[4] As frightening as these drugs sound, they are not the most common substances associated with date rape. About 60 percent of women reporting date rape also report voluntarily consuming alcohol or drugs.[5]

The following story from eighteen-year-old Meagan shows how a rapist might use drugs to incapacitate a victim in order to assault her:

When people think about rape, they never think that it could happen to them. Neither did I, neither did the millions of other survivors. You always think, I know how to avoid those situations, or I would scream. Everyone has an idea of what they would have done but very few actually do that. I froze. I just let it happen. It was like I was paralyzed and I couldn't move, or yell, or even breathe for that matter. I literally froze. A part of me

Questions for Your College

When starting college, or even when considering what college to go to, taking into account the school's response to sexual violence is a good idea. You may need the information later, for yourself or for a friend.

Here are some good questions for your college:

1. What education or prevention programs does the school offer?

   Under the new Clery Act regulations, schools are required to provide education and information on bystander intervention, risk reduction, and reporting practices.

2. What is the reporting process for sexual assault?

   There should be clear, accessible information available on how to report a sexual assault, including confidential reporting, along with what procedures will then be followed.

3. What services are available to students?

   This one goes beyond sexual assault. It's important to know if your school offers counseling or mental health services, housing assistance, victim advocacy, legal assistance, and so on. Often these services are available at little or no additional cost. Your tuition is going toward these programs, so it's good to use them if you need them.[a]

will always hate myself for that. I should have fought back. I should have screamed. There are a million different things that I should have done. But the past is in the past and now I just need to focus on healing.

I had met him just three days before. In the senior cafeteria. He was sweet and flirted a lot. He talked to me about coding and weed and lots of other interesting stuff. His name was Steven. After only a few minutes he asked me for my number and talked about hanging out sometime. He told me I was pretty and he saw me as girlfriend material. I had just gotten out of a horrible relationship so a guy being nice to me was a welcome change. Almost immediately after he left he texted me and once again talked about hanging out. Only after a few short hours of talking that day he was al-

Often college involves an active social life and the consumption of alcohol. Sexual predators tend to take advantage of this environment.

ready calling me "his queen" and saying how beautiful and amazing I was. In theory my red flag should have gone up there but when you're in high school things move very fast sometimes.

During the time while we were "talking" he kept reiterating that we needed to hang out. He said he wanted to get to know me outside of school. He kept calling me his queen and sweet talking me until finally I said yes to hanging out. We decided to go on a walk on a path in the woods near our houses. He told me he would meet me at my house first and we could walk from there since it was closer. My parents had gone out of town for a softball tournament but I didn't think anything of it since we weren't planning on hanging out at my house. I still didn't realize anything was out of the ordinary when he talked me into using my restroom before we left for our walk.

I let him use our guest bathroom in the front hallway of our townhouse since it was the only one clean. While he was in there I was patiently waiting on the couch in the living room, I just kept thinking about how I didn't want to mess this up because it seemed like no guy had even looked at me before like he did. And in all honesty they hadn't. He looked at me like a piece of meat I later realized. He never cared about me or wanted me to actually be his "queen." I was still dumb enough to not think anything was wrong when he started talking about the weed he brought. He convinced me that we should smoke it at my house before our walk in case anyone smelled it on us and called the cops on the trail. I was so gullible. We then went down to the basement and out onto the lower back porch to smoke. With every hit he called me a different nasty name and egged me on to take bigger hits. He used a tone in his voice that made me feel like he was joking, so of course I happily went along with everything. After we finished I realized that he only took half the amount of hits that I did. Even then my red flag was only half way up but I could have never imagined what happened next.

He asked where my room was, and I was kind of relieved that he asked because I felt really weird. I felt light headed and dizzy and my stomach hurt. So of course lying down in my bed sounded great at the time but I guess I had thought that he would leave. Instead he helped me walk inside. My sister and I shared the basement which was split in half by some wardrobes that my dad built. I made it only two steps in the door before I started to stumble and of course he was right there to catch me. I will always remember what he said to me next. This is when my red flag really went up. He said while laughing "Wow you're really messed up aren't you?" I was at a point where I couldn't even respond and yet I still remember everything clear as day. It was like my mind was fully there but my body wasn't.

We still don't know what he had laced the pot with. But what I do know is that he went into my room and decided to make himself right at home on my bed. He laid down and got under the blankets and picked up my tablet and turned on Netflix. At this point I was sitting on my floor trying to think about a way to get him out of there. I just wanted him gone. The room felt so cold and I just wanted to pass out. I slowly stood up while shaking like a Chihuahua from it being freezing in there. I tried to explain that my parents would be home soon and he should get going. All he said was, "You look so cold, here come warm up," and he pulled me onto the bed and very quickly put the blanket over me. He wrapped his arms around me and began to kiss my neck. I had no clue what to do. I didn't kiss him back or say anything. It felt like I wasn't even in my own body. He moved his hand down my body from my shoulder to my hip to my calf where the bottom of my dress sat. The he slowly worked his way back up, bringing the hem of my dress with him. When it was at my hip he moved his hand to touch me. He noted that I wasn't wearing any underwear, which I normally don't do with that dress because of the lines they make. He called me a dirty girl because of that. Almost seconds later he was on top of me, he moved to be in between my legs and he started kissing my breast over my dress and then yanked my dress down forcefully to kiss my skin. After that it was all a blur, things seemed to be in hyper speed. All I could focus on was his breathing. He was grunting like a pig and breathing heavy enough that he could fill a hot air balloon and it would fly with no issue. Luckily it was over quick. He pulled out before he came and it was all over my sheets. He never even fully took his pants off. He just unzipped the zipper. I only know that because he did it back up as he stood up and started to leave. I was still numb and didn't know what to think. All I could think to say was to tell him to leave out the back just in case my parents had just gotten home.

I have no clue how long I laid in bed for. I do know at some point I couldn't stop looking at the stain so I rolled to the floor. Sometime a while later I felt okay enough to get up and change my clothes. I took them right to the wash and I got in the shower. I felt so nasty. We never even talked about sex in the short amount of time that we talked. I didn't know how many people he had been with or if he would go and tell everyone. All I knew from watching *Law & Order* all my life was that if one day I decided to come forward to have some kind of DNA from him. Sadly I didn't think about that until after I showered and washed my clothes but I did leave my sheets.

For two weeks I acted like everything was normal around my family while at night I slept on the floor next to my bed because I didn't want to mess anything up. I was so scared. People did notice a difference even though I thought I was acting normal. My grades dropped, I stopped talking to my friends, I stayed in my room all the time. I didn't want to live anymore. But for some reason a part of me always made sure I didn't wash those sheets. I wanted to so badly though. I had an argument in my head every night about that. Eventually my therapist pried it out of me. I didn't know it was rape even. I just thought it was sex gone bad. To this day I still have trouble saying the word rape in correlation to what happened to me. But that's exactly what it was. Rape. I was raped and now here I am, over a year later. I am standing strong. The police were no help because of how long I waited and my school wasn't either. But here I am. I have been called a whore and a liar. I have been told that I am disgusting and I have no friends. Yet here I am still standing. I am now closer than ever to my family. I have an amazing boyfriend who is so understanding and loving towards my PTSD. And now I'm here to tell you that you are not alone. On my journey I have learned that there are survivors everywhere. You will never be alone and you are strong.[6]

False Beliefs about Date Rape

Is it rape if both people are drunk? Is it rape if someone is too drunk to say no? If the perpetrator has just paid for an expensive date? If the two people have fooled around or had sex before? The answer to all of these questions is yes.

What about False Reports of Rape?

A very common rape myth is that women who claim they were raped are often lying. These women are supposedly "crying rape" to get attention or to get back at a guy. In November 2014, *Rolling Stone* published a sensational article about a particularly brutal gang rape of a student at a fraternity house. Later it was discovered that this story was false; the alleged victim had made the whole thing up, and the journalist who reported the story did not verify the facts. Activists fear that this false report will serve to substantiate the myth that women lie about being raped, and will cause survivors of sexual assault to be even more fearful about reporting the crime.[b]

There have been multiple articles published trying to estimate the rate of false reports. One published in 1994 looked at the reports at one police station over a nine-year period, and saw that 41 percent of them were labeled as false. However, none of those reports were actually investigated, and the practice of that police station at that time was to polygraph rape victims. Rape victims are often easily intimidated, and may recant when treated with hostility. So that report was debunked as being inaccurate and a reflection of that police station's biases against victims of rape rather than a realistic estimate of false reports.

The most up-to-date research indicates that the actual percentage of false reports is between 2 and 8 percent. This is similar to the rates of false reports of all crimes. So why do so many people think that victims are lying about being sexually assaulted?

Part of the reason rape victims are viewed with suspicion is the media portrayal of popular celebrities or sports stars after they are accused of rape. Often there is a statement made by the celebrity, claiming innocence or a misunderstanding. The victim's past is made public, examined, and criticized, leading to complete vilification of the person claiming abuse.

Public perceptions that rape reports are fake may also be impacted by popular rape myths or beliefs. If the victim doesn't "look" like the ideal victim, if the perpetrator seems like a nice guy, if the two people knew each other prior to the assault, if they dated, if they had had consensual sex before . . . all of these can lead an outside observer to think it's not rape.[c]

Will the highly publicized *Rolling Stone* article ultimately hurt rape victims? Unfortunately, it is likely that this incident will serve as confirmation for those who believe that rape victims lie.

In many states, a person can't legally consent to sex if he or she is intoxicated.[7] And while it's always safe to assume that if a person is too drunk to give consent, he or she doesn't consent, some states, such as California and New York, have a new "yes means yes" standard for sex between students at state universities. Basically, for sex to be consensual, both parties have to say yes. Saying nothing is not consent.[8]

Some people, both male and female, believe that if a guy pays for an expensive date, then he's justified in expecting sex.[9] But regardless of how much a date costs, going on a date does not equal giving consent. Consent isn't automatic even if both parties have previously engaged in consensual sex.

Sometimes survivors of sexual assault believe rape myths too. Sometimes a survivor may feel that she is to blame for the assault because of poor choices she may have made. The following story from Taysa, age twenty-four, shows a date rape victim expressing self-blame:

When I was seventeen years old I broke up with my first serious boyfriend. A friend of mine invited me to a hotel party nearby, and I agreed to go.

Once I arrived there were two older guys there. I recognized them, one being a long-time crush of my best friend. They said that other people were on their way and we should start drinking. As a teenager and not really understanding the repercussions that could come from this situation, I did. There was a lot of pressure to keep drinking from all three of them (my friend and the two guys) and eventually I ended up spending hours throwing up in the bathroom. I came back into the room and went to the bed where my friend and one guy were not hooking up in. This is when I realized that no one else was coming . . . that there was no one else to begin with.

Still drunk, I passed out on the bed opposite to my friend. Not long after I woke up to my head being held down as one of the guys forced me to give him oral. I didn't know what to do. I tried to say something and move away but I was so incredibly disoriented that I couldn't. My friend must have fallen asleep or something because not long after the other guy came behind me. At that point I was scared for my life. I just closed my eyes and eventually passed out. When I woke up it was morning and they were gone. They had written a note on one of the hotel notepads. They took the note with them, but you could read the imprint on the one below it saying "thanks for the good time." My friend laughed about it. I was disgusted, but I felt so much guilt that I just went along with her.

For so many years I convinced myself that it was my fault and that I deserved it. But I didn't. I know that I didn't. I know that I made a mistake in walking into that hotel room, but walking in was not an invitation to my body.[10]

What Can Bystanders Do?

One thing that research on these kinds of sexual assaults has uncovered is that sexual assaults are usually committed by repeat offenders. Because the prosecution rate for rape is so low, these predators remain free in society and can continue to assault people.[11] Because of this, more and more universities are finding it helpful to train students to help as bystanders rather than giving the traditional "sexual assault is wrong" lecture.[12] But what can bystanders do to prevent sexual assault?

Many of these types of programs involve role-playing exercises and brainstorming ways to defuse a tense situation. Distraction techniques are suggested, like interrupting a conversation and turning the lights up or the music off. The goal is to make preventing sexual assault everyone's business. Little research has been done to find out how effective these programs are, but every assault they prevent is a win.[13]

Prevention Training and the Controversy about It

In 2015 a research team published the result of a research project in the *New England Journal of Medicine*. The team had recruited two groups of college women from three universities in Canada. One group was given pamphlets about the risks of sexual assault and information about services available to victims. The other group was given intensive prevention training, including self-defense, guidance on how to determine sexual boundaries, role-playing to increase communication skills in a potentially dangerous situation, and risk-reduction guidelines. A year later, the team surveyed the two groups, and found that the group of women who had gone through prevention training were much less likely to be the victims of rape or of an attempted rape.[14]

Sounds great, right? What could be wrong with a program that's been proven to reduce the risk of being sexually assaulted?

There are actually a lot of concerns about programs that focus on prevention training. One concern is that a perpetrator, when confronted by a difficult target, will just move on to an easier victim. Another, larger concern is that by focusing on prevention training, the focus and responsibility for the sexual assault is being shifted from the perpetrator to the victim, which for some advocates sounds a lot like victim blaming.[15]

Sexual Assault Education Should Begin before College

While college-age women are at high risk of being sexually assaulted, 40 percent of women who report being raped were first assaulted when they were under eighteen. As illustrated by the first two stories in this chapter, high school

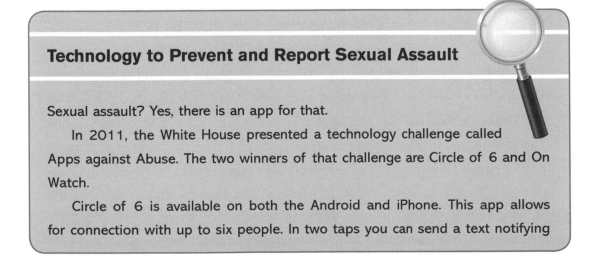

Technology to Prevent and Report Sexual Assault

Sexual assault? Yes, there is an app for that.

In 2011, the White House presented a technology challenge called Apps against Abuse. The two winners of that challenge are Circle of 6 and On Watch.

Circle of 6 is available on both the Android and iPhone. This app allows for connection with up to six people. In two taps you can send a text notifying your group that you need help or need someone to interrupt a situation. It also has GPS tracking so you can be found if needed, and provides connection with reputable domestic violence organizations.[d]

On Watch is only available on an iPhone. It has some great features, like a timer to notify friends if you're out alone and don't make it back when you expect to. If the timer runs out and you don't respond, On Watch sends an automatic notification to your friends with your GPS location. It also offers arrival notifications to let friends know you've arrived at your destination safely. However, all of these features require a subscription. The app does offer a button to quickly call campus police or 911, and there is a free thirty-day trial for the additional services.[e]

While these two apps did win the White House challenge, they are not the only apps designed to keep people, especially college students, safe. One app that is commonly used by college campuses is LiveSafe.

LiveSafe, which was created by a survivor of the 2007 Virginia Tech shooting, is available on iPhone and Android. LiveSafe was designed for reporting all types of campus crime, not just sexual assault. It allows for anonymous reporting, which could be appealing for some sexual assault survivors. It also sends direct alerts to your phone from your college about safety concerns. On the Go Safe option, you can request campus security to give you a ride to your car if you're uncomfortable walking alone, or you can enable GPS tracking that allows a friend or several friends to watch your progress and ensure you arrive safely. It also provides quick links to call campus police.[f]

Off phone and online, another great resource for survivors is Callisto. Callisto allows the survivor of a sexual assault to record the event. The record is private and is only sent to the school's Title IX coordinator when you decide to submit a report. Another option is available if you know the perpetrator. You can set the record to be submitted automatically if someone else writes a report identifying that same perpetrator. Follow-up and support services are also offered. Callisto is still in development and is not available on all campuses. However, on the Callisto website you can request for it to be available at your campus. Even though Callisto is not widely available at this time, the website still provides many valuable resources for survivors. The Callisto website is www.projectcallisto.org.

students are in danger of date rape as well. Programs in Illinois and New York middle schools have proven effective in preventing sexual harassment in school, and researchers are beginning to look at how sexual health education could help prevent assault.[16]

Many victims of sexual assault, including date rape victims, lack the language to define what has happened to them. These victims still imagine rape as being the stranger who jumps out at them from a dark alley at night. When the assault comes from a friend, when there's alcohol involved, when the victim doesn't understand what sexual assault is, the victim is more likely to blame him- or herself, more likely to not report, and more likely not to seek help. Additionally, an educational campaign in high school or middle school could provide potential victims as well as bystanders the skills to prevent assault. And by educating would-be assailants about consent and healthy sexual relationships, it may possibly prevent them from initiating sexual violence in the first place.

Why Do Campus Hearings Seem Weighted against the Accused?

In an episode from season 6 of *The Good Wife*, which aired on CBS in November 2014, attorney Alicia Florrick is called upon to assist the victim of sexual assault at a campus disciplinary hearing. In the episode, the victim is badgered by the accused during the hearing, and little that she says is believed. When she tries to tell the story of what happened to her, she's interrupted multiple times by the young man accused of assaulting her. When Alicia tries to intervene, the professor in charge (it's emphasized that he's just a professor and not trained to work with assault victims) interrupts Alicia, informing her that the disciplinary hearing is not a court case. The script follows the narrative often heard from victims of campus sexual assault who say their cases were mishandled by the college disciplinary hearings.[9] This particular TV series usually incorporates current events and legal debates into the plot of the program. The usage of the campus sexual assault debate is no exception to this trend: in 2014, there were ninety-six Title IX complaints filed with the Department of Education that were related to sexual violence. That same year there were more than eighty-five colleges under investigation for not doing enough to address sexual assault.[h] Because of this increased reporting, colleges are starting to reform how they are addressing reports of sexual assault.

However, there are some who say that the real victim of the amplified efforts to punish rapists is not the one claiming to have been sexually assaulted; to some the real victim is the accused. In October 2014, twenty-eight members of the Harvard Law School faculty published an open letter condemning Harvard's sexual misconduct policies, for not providing the accused with due process or adequate representation. The Harvard Law School faculty members aren't the only ones raising concerns about college disciplinary councils.[i]

A group of concerned family members of college men accused of sexual assault have formed an advocacy group called Families Advocating for Campus Equality (FACE). The stated mission of FACE is to provide outreach and education to families who are dealing with campus disciplinary hearings for sexual assault. The website highlights news articles about campus justice gone wrong and college faculty members speaking out against disciplinary hearings.[j] Many of those who argue against the current system of college disciplinary hearings wish to see all such cases handled by the legal system rather than by colleges.

Those who push for campuses to address sexual assault point out that such hearings can help victims by immediately separating them from the accused. It is also of note that the punishments meted out by these councils are not the same as those given in a court of law. Often they involve community service. Sometimes the punishment seems completely pointless. In 2014, James Madison University (JMU) found three fraternity brothers guilty of sexually assaulting a female student and posting a video of it online; the punishment was "expulsion after graduation," meaning that their punishment dictated that they never return to campus after graduating. JMU was later sued for this decision.[k]

While a lot of focus has been given to men who claim they were falsely accused of rape, statistically a man is more likely to be raped on a college campus than he is to be falsely accused of rape.[l]

Given the history of sexual assault on college campuses, the new leaning toward believing the victim is seen by many feminists to compensate for social biases and rape myths, including victim blaming. There does not seem to be a simple solution to this nuanced and complex problem.

The Legal Debate: How Should Colleges Handle Sexual Misconduct?

Colleges and universities have recently been under pressure to improve the way they handle sexual assault cases. In September 2014, President Barack Obama announced a public awareness campaign, "It's on Us," with the goal of preventing sexual violence on college campuses in the United States.[17] There are currently two major federal laws that dictate how campuses should handle allegations of sexual misconduct or assault. They are Title IX and the Clery Act.[18]

Among other protections, these federal laws require schools to hold disciplinary hearings. The maximum punishment such a hearing can decide is expulsion. Advocates see this as justice, because then the person who has been assaulted can continue going to school away from the person who assaulted him or her. Because

Consent cannot be given by a person who is intoxicated or incapacitated.

court cases can take years to be decided, a school expulsion is also a way to protect other students on campus from a sexual predator. This is action that can be taken in addition to or instead of legal prosecution. Some feel, however, that college courts are unfair to the accused. The burden of proof is less, and the panel only has to believe it to be 51 percent likely that an assault was committed. Others feel that expulsion is too harsh a punishment. The question is how accountable should universities hold students for their actions.[19]

Affirmative Consent Policies

Another approach that colleges are taking to clear up misunderstandings about sexual assault is establishing affirmative consent policies. Previous campus standards required victims to prove they had said no. Because of the tendency of rape victims to freeze during a sexual assault, requiring vocalized consent at each stage of sexual intimacy ensures that no one is engaging in something he or she is not comfortable with. Advocates also point out the importance of clear communication about sexual wants. Learning to communicate about sex is a lifelong skill. Since freezing is common and since a person cannot say no if incapacitated, the yes means yes standards provide clarification for assault hearings. California and New York State have both made yes means yes the standard for college campuses, and many colleges across the nation are beginning to adopt this standard.[20]

Getting Help

The time period immediately following a sexual assault can be very confusing. You may be unsure of what has happened to you. You may want some guidance as to what your options are. Going to the police or the hospital by yourself may also be intimidating, even if you do wish to report the crime. Your local rape crisis center can provide guidance, counseling services, and advocates to accompany you to the hospital or police, even to court should your case lead to legal action. You can look up your local crisis center at www.centers.rainn.org. You can also call an anonymous hotline at 1-800-656-HOPE (4673), which will route you to trained staff at a local rape crisis center. There is also an online chat available at ohl.rainn.org/online/. These are all services coordinated through the Rape, Abuse and Incest National Network (www.rainn.org).

If you have been, or think you have been, the victim of a date rape and you wish to report, it's important to go to the hospital as soon as you can. Do not wash or change clothes. The hospital will need to gather evidence from your clothing. Once you're at the hospital, you will also be checked for sexually transmitted dis-

The Hunting Ground Raises Awareness of Campus Assault

While director Kirby Dick and producer Amy Ziering were traveling the country visiting college campuses to do screenings of their 2011 documentary *The Invisible War*, which is about sexual assault in the armed forces, they were surprised by the number of college women who approached them after the screening to disclose having similar experiences of being sexually assaulted as students. This led the two to look closely at campus sexual assault, which led to the creation of *The Hunting Ground*.

The Hunting Ground looks at the experiences of several victims of sexual assault from different campuses across the country. It also includes interviews with law enforcement and psychologists to examine more closely the concerns and ramifications of how reports of sexual assault were handled by universities.

One incident that the film examines is Florida State University's handling of the sexual assault allegation against its star quarterback, Jameis Winston. University president John Thrasher did not like the documentary's portrayal of Florida State and publicly criticized the film. Kirby Dick and Amy Ziering issued the following open letter to President Thrasher, which was originally published in the *Huffington Post* in November 2015:

An Open Letter to Florida State University President Thrasher,

We respectfully but emphatically disagree with your criticisms of our film *The Hunting Ground*. Instead of making unwarranted and unsubstantiated attacks on the film, we urge you to take a leadership role in addressing the problem of sexual assault that exists on your campus and far too many others.

The film is completely accurate in its depiction of Ms. Kinsman's account, and its depiction of how her case was handled by Florida State University.

You say there are distortions and glaring omissions, yet you are not able to state a single factual error in our film. That is because there are none.

Your assertion that the film did not mention Jameis Winston's Title IX investigation, or its outcome, is not true. Both are mentioned in the film.

You say FSU is a "model" when it comes to handling sexual assault. The truth is that your school is being investigated by the Department of Education for its mishandling of sexual assault cases, and many media outlets, including The New York Times, have detailed how your school covered up sexual assault allegations against its former star quarterback.

In an interview on January 16, 2015, you said FSU has been "aggressively" working on a "scheme" regarding the negative publicity FSU has received about how they mishandled Title IX complaints. Rather than scheming, we believe FSU students are better served by efforts to make their campus safe.

You claim FSU "did everything appropriately" in regard to Erica Kinsman's Title IX complaint. We believe the facts show otherwise:

- December 7, 2012—Kinsman immediately reported her rape to the Florida State University and Tallahassee police within hours of the assault. She was taken to a nearby hospital where a rape kit was administered and bruises were noted in her medical record. FSU police did not report the assault to the FSU Title IX Coordinator as required by federal guidelines.
- January 22, 2013—Florida State Head Football Coach Jimbo Fisher learned that Jameis Winston had been accused of sexual assault but did not report the assault to the FSU Title IX Coordinator as required by federal guidelines.
- For the next eighteen months, FSU did almost nothing to investigate this report of rape even though the FSU school policy and the Department of Education presumes that any accusation of sexual assault will be investigated and resolved within 60 days.
- November 12, 2013—Despite being on notice that another female FSU student had reported being sexually assaulted by Winston, FSU stated in an email that no disciplinary proceedings against Winston were going to take place for either of the reported assaults.

- November 14, 2013—Kinsman dropped out of school, fearing for her safety because of retaliation over social media from FSU students and fans.
- December 14, 2013—Winston was named winner of the 2013 Heisman Trophy.
- January 6, 2014—FSU's football team won the BCS National Championship.
- January 23, 2014—More than a year after FSU officials were made aware that Winston was accused of rape, FSU finally called Winston in for an interview regarding the accusation. Winston refused to answer any questions. After the interview, FSU sent a letter to Winston stating they were not going to investigate the case because Winston refused to talk to them.
- In the spring of 2014—FSU, in violation of the victim advocate privilege, gave a copy of Kinsman's privileged victim advocate file to its outside legal counsel.
- December 5, 2014—Nearly two years after the report of rape, FSU finally held a hearing about the accusation. The FSU hearing officer found Winston not responsible despite the fact he refused to answer every question put to him by the hearing officer except three while Kinsman answered all 156 questions asked of her.
- January 7, 2015—Six days after his final football game, Winston withdrew from FSU and made himself eligible for the 2015 NFL Football Draft.

I would strongly encourage you to respond to the crisis on our campuses in the spirit of Harvard's President Drew Faust. In a letter dated September 21 to the Harvard community, she said: "The prevalence of sexual assault represents a deeply troubling problem for Harvard . . . but the difficulty and severity of the problem make it all the more important that we come together to address it."

FSU students are best served by an administration that acknowledges past mistakes and focuses on the very real problem of sexual assault on its campus.

Best Regards,
Kirby Dick, Director
Amy Ziering, Producer
*The Hunting Ground*ᵐ

I was fortunate enough to get in touch with Amy Ziering, the producer of *The Hunting Ground*, and she was kind enough to answer a few questions about this documentary:

Q: *Was this film in response to a perceived need?*

When we screened *The Invisible War* on college campuses, time and again, students would tell us that the sexual assault issues in the military were similar to what they'd experienced at their colleges and universities when they'd reported an assault. We started doing our own investigating and found out the problems were pervasive and systemic on campuses throughout the U.S.—and that colleges and universities, rather than addressing the problem, were covering it up.

We began filming nearly a year before the issue became widely known to the public, undertaking one of the most extensive investigations ever into college sexual assault, and captured the rise of a new student movement as it was unfolding in real time.

Q: *What hopes do you have for this documentary?*

Our last film, *The Invisible War*, led to the penning and passing of thirty-five pieces of legislation, and then Secretary of Defense Leon Panetta's holding of a press conference two days after viewing, to announce significant changes to Pentagon policy. Similarly, in addition to garnering awards and much critical acclaim, *The Hunting Ground* has had an extraordinary impact on the sexual assault dialogue on college campuses nationwide. The film has screened at over 1,000 universities, high schools, community centers, and government offices across the country—sparking long silenced debate and policy change school by school. In October 2015, Chancellor Mike Powers of the University of Alaska, Fairbanks—post a screening of *The Hunting Ground* on his campus—became the first college president in history to publicly apologize to survivors and the community for his institutions mishandling and negligence of sexual assault crimes. He attributed these actions directly to his having watched the film.

The film has had high profile screenings at the White House, Department of Justice, Office of Civil Rights, Department of Education, ESPN, and the NCAA. To date, more than fifteen pieces of legislation have been written in four different state legislatures. In the wake of the film's screening for key delegates in New York, Governor Andrew Cuomo was able to swiftly pass Enough Is Enough—a new bill combating sexual assault on NY college campuses. Globally, the film has instigated campaigns to combat sexual violence on campuses, recently raising one million dollars in Australia to support screenings and outreach efforts there. Efforts are underway to launch similar campaigns in the U.K. and France. Recently, the film team partnered with director Catherine Hardwicke to release a powerful and moving short film about college sexual assault based on the original song by Lady Gaga featured in *The Hunting Ground*—this short film has already received over twenty-five million views.

We think our film is doing a lot towards changing hearts and minds, especially of men—many of whom have never considered this issue from the perspective of assault survivors. Men often come up to us after screenings and thank us for making the film and say that it helped them better understand the nature and impact of these crimes. Many have gone so far as to say that it completely changed their perspective on rape. They had believed many of the predominating rape myths that suggest "women lie" when reporting. Our film and studies show that the likelihood that someone is lying about this crime is actually not only extremely low, but also statistically consistent with the likelihood that one is lying when reporting any other crime in our society. Yet you never hear anyone asking someone who reports a robbery: "Are you sure you didn't mean to give him your television set?" or "What were you wearing when you say he took your TV?"

Q: What would you like to see for victims of sexual assault?

First, I would like to have campuses own this issue and take it seriously in a way that's not just rhetorical. Have them finally say: "okay—this is happening, and we're really going to better respond to survivors and properly investigate and adjudicate these crimes." That would mean have processes in place that are fair to both the accused and accuser, and that better assesses these crimes and remove persons who may be threats to others on campus. And then, I'd like to see a whole cultural transformation in which survivors are better understood and supported. The good news is campuses are already well-resourced—they just would need to better allocate their resources so that more money is spent on staffing and training their women's centers, therapists, Title IX coordinators, assault adjudicators, etc. This is not an insoluble problem. We can fix this.

Additionally, I'd like for survivors to know that if this happens to them, it is never ever their fault. They should not blame themselves—it is not their fault—they are victims of a violent crime. And there was, in almost all the cases I heard, nothing anyone could have done in any way shape or form to have changed the outcome of the circumstances. More often than not these are premeditated crimes—we like to call them target rape as opposed to date rape. And the fault and blame lies squarely and entirely on the perpetrator. That's super important for survivors to understand, and also for parents of survivors to understand that they should not blame their child.[n]

Lady Gaga's song from *The Hunting Ground*, "Til It Happens to You," was co-written by Diane Warren. The song was nominated for an Oscar in 2016. At the Oscars that year, Lady Gaga, first introduced by Vice President Joe Biden, powerfully performed the song at a piano. At the end of the performance she was joined on stage by a large group of sexual assault survivors, with words about their experiences written on their arms. The performance earned a standing ovation.[o]

---

eases (STDs). A doctor may prescribe treatment to prevent you from developing an STD.

If more than seventy-two hours have passed since you were assaulted, you can still go to the police to report the rape. Or you can go to a local rape crisis center for help. The sooner you report a rape, the better, but you can report rapes months or sometimes even years afterward.[21]

Unfortunately, victims of sexual assault do not always have the language to communicate or the words to identify what has happened to them. This can be compounded when drugs or alcohol are involved in the assault. Training for medical personal and others to identify the signs of sexual trauma may help victims like the one in the following story. At one point in this story, the anonymous writer mentions becoming separated from the new friends who were supposed to be looking out for her. This is an example of a time when an app like Circle of 6 would come in handy. In addition, the perpetrator uses manipulation to downplay the assault and to convince this survivor that what had happened wasn't sexual assault:

> It happened in college, at one of the first parties I'd been to in my entire life. I was a freshman, thrilled at my newfound friends and the euphoria of starting life living on my own. My friends and I had made a vague pact to watch out for each other and stay together. Later, they said they didn't know how they'd lost me. They just couldn't find me.
>
> I was already pretty drunk by the time I started dancing with a particular guy who I'd met briefly at an earlier party. As the night progressed, the guy I was with kept giving me drinks, at one point tilting an unasked-for strong drink into my mouth.
>
> He walked me to his room, helping me stay upright because I was so unsteady, and I went along with zero thoughts at all running through my hazy mind. The sexual assault itself was an out-of-body experience. I don't know how much that had to do with the shock itself or how much was the amount of alcohol in my system. At one point, I vomited. Years later, I'm grateful to be alive—not because this particular perpetrator would have killed me, but because I could have died of alcohol poisoning.
>
> The numbness stayed, though, even after the alcohol had worn off.
>
> Even after I was back in my dorm room.
>
> Even after I took a shower.
>
> Even when I went to the campus health center for help the next day because I was so battered and bruised in and around my pelvis that I couldn't ride my bike to classes. The nurse gasped during my checkup and then told me, "It's better if the woman is aroused during intercourse."
>
> You see, I hadn't said it was sexual assault. I didn't know it was sexual assault—perhaps because I had never heard of sexual assault of an incapacitated person. After all, I hadn't said no. And the little I knew about sexual assault revolved around the phrase "no means no." Or perhaps the denial was just too numbing for me to process what had happened. I wasn't actively thinking about the assault—or much of anything at all. In retrospect, I think I was waiting for someone to define it for me, to tell me what had happened to me. Which is why I went into that medical clinic, but then didn't really say what had happened.

Later on, still during the day after, the perpetrator called me, his voice nervous. He'd had to wash his sheets, he said, because there was blood all over them. Why had I done that, he wanted to know. Why had I gone back to his room and had sex with him? He wanted to meet with me, and I agreed to do so. Why *had* I done that? He made me want to know why too. And so began the brainwashing. It got so bad that I convinced myself I was actually seeing him—to the point of letting him have sex with me again (not my idea, but consensual in this case). As he relaxed with my willingness to go along with everything, he started telling me about other close calls he'd had: plagiarizing papers, stealing a jeep one time while drunk, and . . . getting accused of sexual assault by another young woman on campus.

In the meantime, I was in a posttraumatic state, but didn't realize it. I was failing tests because time felt different—not to mention that I had no concentration at all. I had an exaggerated startle response. I was scared to sleep in a room alone. At one point later in the year, I had a flashback while making out with my new boyfriend.

By this point, I knew on some level that I had been sexually assaulted back in the fall. However, I was ashamed of everything about it: I felt stupid for having been "duped" with drinks in the first place, I felt that I hadn't acted correctly during the assault because of not resisting, and I felt that I'd lost all credibility by going back to the perpetrator—even though I actually did understand why I'd chosen that version of events as preferable to dealing with reality.

I did get another physical exam—because I was having pain from scar tissue—and a battery of tests for STDs the summer after the assault.

But I didn't deal with the psychological consequences of what had happened to me. I wasn't ready to do so for another fifteen years—not until I was into my thirties with two kids—at which point I entered therapy. I learned then that I had chronic PTSD, which explained why, all these years later, I felt uncomfortable around men most of the time. I also still had intrusive thoughts and flashbacks, shame over what had happened, and, as I grew older, regret that I might have stopped him from raping others if I had been "stronger" initially. . . .

When others tell rape jokes or blame survivors for what happened to them, it still feels like those people are directing their comments personally at me. In contrast, the recent heightened awareness of the prevalence of campus assault and the use of alcohol as a weapon has felt directly empowering to me.[22]

Resources for College Victims of Sexual Assault

End Rape on Campus: 1-424-777-3762, www.endrapeoncampus.org
Know Your IX: www.knowyourix.org
The National Center for Victims of Crime: www.victimsofcrime.org
National Sexual Assault Online Hotline: ohl.rainn.org/online/
National Sexual Assault Hotline: 1-800-656-HOPE
Students Active for Ending Rape (SAFER): www.safercampus.org

DATING VIOLENCE AND SEXUAL ASSAULT IN RELATIONSHIPS

Because sexual assault in relationships is usually intertwined with other kinds of dating violence, this chapter will examine some of the aspects of dating violence and how they relate to sexual assault between partners.

What Is Teen Dating Violence?

The term *teen dating violence* encompasses a wide range of abusive behaviors. It includes physical abuse, like hitting, pushing, scratching, biting, hair-pulling, and slapping. It also includes psychological abuse, like insults, threats, name-calling, put-downs, and isolation from friends and family. And it includes sexual abuse.

Sexual abuse in a relationship can include rape, but it's also pressure to have sex, pressure to have oral sex, unwanted touching and kissing, and sexting. Teen dating violence can occur in person, but it can also occur online, through social media, and over the phone or through text messages.

These three kinds of teen dating violence usually occur in connection to one another. For example, violence often starts with psychological abuse, things like name-calling or put-downs—things that can easily be shrugged off or ignored. This can evolve into manipulation and guilt trips to achieve desired behavior. Then it can go one step further, into using manipulation for sex. Or it could evolve into threats and physical violence. Just as every relationship is different, so is every abusive relationship.

Many different kinds of abuse can occur in a relationship. The following story from Alexandra, age twenty-four, gives several examples. Abuse also tends to escalate. Alexandra was later raped by that same ex-boyfriend:

> My ex was cruel, selfish, and controlling. He was good with words, and
> would spend hours talking to me and convincing me of things (including

to date him). The first time we broke up was around our two year mark, and it was mutual. Afterwards, though, I kept finding out just how sleazy he really was: slapping girl's asses at his own birthday party when I was right there, flirting constantly behind my back, and it only took him two nights to sleep with his ex who "is just like a sister." He tends to keep his ex-girlfriends as best friends, which was part of the issue. I caught him saying sexual things to that one ex before we broke up. He was right next to me (arm and arm) texting her, all I had to do was look over. I couldn't stand the person he was. I wasn't a jealous person, and he trained me to be. He told me the ridiculous things he did purposely just to make me jealous. I didn't want anything to do with him. I kept him at a distance but we still were "friends." When I really got sick of him, I tried to break contact with him completely. I went off the grid for a week without telling anyone and he freaked out. He loved to guilt me in any argument and turn everything around on me. Even if I was the one he deliberately hurt, I had to learn to not let him walk over me like that and catch him the moment he was being unfair, or it wouldn't matter later.[1]

The statistics from the recent survey on teen dating violence performed by NORC at the University of Chicago indicate that close to 20 percent of teens are victims of physical and sexual abuse in dating relationships, and that over 60 percent have experienced psychological abuse in dating relationships.[2] In other studies there have been some slight variations in who is abusing who and in the kind of abuse, but it's important to note that both males and females are victims of teen dating violence and of sexual assault in relationships.[3] Also teens in LGBTQ (lesbian, gay, bisexual, transgender, queer/questioning) relationships are just as likely to experience dating violence and sexual assault as straight couples.[4] Because of these facts, this chapter will discuss dating violence and sexual assault in a gender-neutral way.

Sexual Coercion

Sexual coercion is a term used to describe one partner pressuring the other for sex or for the other partner to perform sexual acts.

Why do teens sometimes agree to sexual acts they aren't comfortable with? How is sexual coercion effective?

Teens give in to sexual pressure for several reasons. They may have unwanted sex as a way to show their partner that they love them, or because they fear a breakup. Alcohol and drug use can play a part. Teens may decide to have sex or perform sexual acts because they think their friends are doing it too.[5]

⍰ Is Your Relationship Healthy?

Healthy relationships contain several elements. Respect and boundaries are two of the most important. Does your partner

- get mad or upset when you spend time with friends?
- insist on knowing your online log-ins?
- read your emails or texts without permission?
- call or text late at night after you've asked the person not to?
- send excessive numbers of text messages?
- want to know your whereabouts at all times?
- make mean comments about you online?
- become jealous easily?
- check photos on your phone?
- try to make you send sexual texts or pictures when you don't want to?
- threaten to harm you or him- or herself?
- make you afraid for your safety?

If you answer yes to any of these questions, your relationship may be abusive. Remember, these are just a few of the behaviors that are signs of teen dating violence. If your relationship makes you uncomfortable or causes you to feel bad about yourself, you should consider ending it.

The following story from Melinda shows how she felt in an emotional and sexually abusive relationship, and some of the tactics she used to cope with the abuse. Even though the sexual abuse did not involve sex, it was still sexual abuse:

But my thoughts on this have left me feeling shaky and weak: What exactly constitutes rape? If you keep all your clothes on, and you initially consent, but then you want him to get the hell off you because it hurts, and he doesn't until he's done, is that technically rape?

It's not like I'm going to press charges or anything. And it's not like Preston was forcing me to do more, not like he forced me to take off my clothes, it's not like he ever saw me in a state of even partial undress. He was lucky to see my ankles! But there were multiple incidents where I

Inexcusable by Chris Lynch

The young adult novel *Inexcusable* by Chris Lynch looks at sexual assault in teen relationships from the point of view of the perpetrator. A compelling read, it shows how easily abusive and dangerous behaviors can be rationalized or ignored. It also illustrates how abuse can be hidden under a facade.[a]

---

didn't want him to hurt me like that, but he went on and did it anyway. And there was one time in Nodaway when we were making out and he just got on top and did his thing. I take consolation in the fact that his dick was probably rubbed raw each time. But I was pretty sore, too.

I mean, there in the last couple of months, it was just this lustful rampage on my part too. I had come to the conclusion of "what the hell, if he's using me then I'll use him." But the problem was, I preferred staying on top so I could have my fun, but he didn't prefer that. And you know the kicker is that I'd be on top, having my fun, but then he'd roll me over and get on top and just squash the hell out of every good feeling I'd been having. He didn't even wait for me to finish up what I was doing before he'd roll me over! He'd just get on top and start mashing into me, and he's a freaking big guy. I distinctly remember one time telling him, "Stop it, geez, that hurts," but he went right on. And that time in Nodaway, when I was finally able to break away I glared at him. Did he apologize? What did it matter if he did apologize or not, he still did it. . . . All that I could do was hold on and try to bear it and tell him to lighten up. All that I would see was his shoulder and the right side of his head, but not his face. . . .

And I hated him for it! I would hide from him the next day. I'd know when he'd be out and about, so when he was scheduled to come through I'd go into my hidey places and watch him pass by from them, and once I was satisfied he was gone, I'd head on out to my destination. I often would duck into the south stairwell of Garrett-Strong, which had a little window on each flight that I could watch him through, and they were small (and grimy) enough to where my face wouldn't show through. I'd watch him pass by with a sick feeling in my gut, thinking, Why did I do that with him? and I'd feel disgusting and awful, like what had happened last night made me unclean.

I still don't feel like it could be called rape. The definition is (1) sexual (2) intercourse by (3) force. So technically, two out of three. And I was in a relationship—though not by my consent, there is definitely that.

Even the last time we exchanged emails, Preston just said, "Let's split the blame 50/50 and leave it at that," and then he moseyed on to another topic. Actually, I get the idea that he doesn't really blame himself very much. Some kind of weird reality transference that he's good at.

I'm sitting here looking at this tangle of earbud and speaker cords on my desk, and being in that relationship was like being a little bug on one of those cords, following it around and around in that tangle but not being able to find a way out of that mess.

This brings me back to my novel I'm writing. I keep thinking about it. All the stuff that I left out. Stuff like this. I still can't call it rape, even though what happened to me partly fits the definition. There are no real demarcations of what's right or what's wrong, no line that you cross and say, here's the boundary.

What exactly is emotional abuse? There's a lot of grey there, too. At this distance, about twenty-five years later, what I went through doesn't seem all that bad, compared to a lot of other relationships. So you were held against your will for the better part of a year, so what? So he climbed on you a few times and hurt you. So what? So he misrepresents stuff he said to you and misremembers his part in the relationship. He's in the next freaking state. It's not like I was stuck with him for three years, and it's not like he's in the neighborhood stalking me daily. I only think about him because of this story I've written. Maybe I should stop dredging this up and move on and forget about the creep.

But at the same time, these questions are important, because other girls are asking these same questions right now. Other girls are saying, He's not so bad. He does it because he loves me. I just want to go out there and deconstruct all that, right now!

Later I told Brad what I was thinking about today about Preston and the rapey thing. "So what is it?" I asked him. "I don't think it's rape, but at the same time, I don't know what it is."

"It's assault," he said.

It is just marvelous how my confusion instantly dissipated and turned to a huge sense of relief. That makes so much more sense.

It's so good to have someone in your life that just understands stuff so well and can just nail the matter down in a single word.[6]

Myths about Sexual Assault

A few of the many myths about sexual assault are that it doesn't happen in relationships, or that if you've engaged in consensual sex with that partner before, then it can't really be rape or assault later. Another misconception is that sexual coercion, or one partner pressuring the other for sex, is normal. And while males have reported being pressured into sexual activities too, one study of teen interviews found that the prevailing attitude was that guys just want to have sex, they are going to do or say anything so they can get it, and this is normal.[7]

Online Relationships

Most teens are online, have cell phones, and use social media like Facebook, Twitter, and Instagram. With all these ways to stay connected, teens in romantic relationships can be in almost constant contact with each other. Many teens send pictures either through text messages or apps like Snapchat. Others even exchange passwords to email accounts and social media accounts as a token of trust. Is this constant contact a good thing for relationships?

A lot of teens think it is. It's a way to share more time together even when school or home demands keep a couple apart. But many of these behaviors have

Being in a relationship with someone does not automatically grant consent. You can still say no, and if your partner can't accept that, it's probably best to end the relationship.

Stay Connected!

Wondering what the best ways are to avoid an abusive relationship? Most abusive relationships begin with the abuser isolating the victim from friends and family. And recent research shows that teens who have close relationships with family and friends are much less likely to be in abusive romantic relationships. So stay connected to others besides your romantic partner![b]

What are some ways to stay connected? Set clear boundaries with your time. Establish a girls' night out or a guys' movie night, something that gives you a night out with friends and a short break from your significant other. You can also talk to your family about setting aside family time each week or planning a weekend trip together. Suggest to your boyfriend or girlfriend that he or she do the same. Balance is important in healthy relationships, and you should work on keeping all of your relationships strong, including those with friends and family members.

negative consequences, especially password sharing. In one study on teen relationships, teens reported deleting their own text messages, emails, and Facebook messages to avoid having an argument with their partner.[8]

Electronic Pictures

Sexual assault through electronic means includes sending pictures or engaging in phone sex. In one study, about one in four teens reported being pressured into doing something sexual over the phone or the computer that he or she wasn't comfortable doing.[9]

Sharing naked photos is risky for several reasons. The photos could be found on your phone or computer, or on your partner's phone or computer. Your partner could share them without your consent during your relationship or after a breakup as a form of revenge.

Some teens feel safe sending private pictures through an app like Snapchat that allows the recipient to see the image only once and only for a few seconds. However, even with apps like this there is still a risk of the photo being saved. If the recipient is quick, he or she can take a picture of the photo with the phone before it disappears.

With text messages, photos, status updates, tweets, and blog posts it's important to remember that whatever you put out there will stay out there, that a copy can be saved even if you delete your post, and that there is always a risk of others finding or sharing your information.

As with other aspects of teen dating violence, online abuse is interconnected to other aspects of the relationship too. Victims of cyber-dating violence are most likely experiencing other forms of abuse in their dating relationships as well.[10]

Explicit and Implicit Beliefs about Dating Violence

Dating is exciting and should be a fun experience. Why are some relationships punctuated by abuse? Why are some partners unwilling to accept no as an answer?

We have two sets of beliefs that impact our behavior. The first is called *explicit knowledge*, what we consciously know and believe. The second is our *implicit knowledge*, what we subconsciously know and believe. Having this dual belief system explains why someone who says he thinks or believes one thing may act in a way different from it. It's also why someone who says that she or he is sorry and will change, may change the behavior for a while, and then revert back to old patterns of abuse. These teens are not actually lying; their explicit knowledge, or conscious beliefs, have changed. Changes to one's conscious beliefs about abuse in relationships can occur from reading an informative article, from talking with friends, from seeing the harm caused by abusive behavior, or from fear of the relationship ending. Unfortunately, our subconscious beliefs do not change so easily and may take more work to override. Changes to subconscious beliefs may occur after seeking counseling or the help of other professionals, or after years of self-monitoring and education on the issue of abuse.[11]

The subconscious or implicit beliefs of the abuser can impact his or her split-second decisions. The individual may lash out in anger at an initial threat, like the partner receiving a text message from an old boyfriend or girlfriend. Later the individual may recognize that the initial reaction was not appropriate and will most likely apologize. However, because it's so hard to change implicit beliefs, the individual will most likely overreact again should a similar event occur.

Being the victim of a sexual assault can cause an individual to have low self-esteem and feelings of little self-worth. These individuals are then more likely to be in abusive or dangerous relationships. Implicit beliefs about what abuse looks like and what sexual assault looks like can also impact the way someone reacts to abuse. In the following story, Lindsay was raped at a party when she was fifteen but did not get help. Instead she suppressed and down-played the incident as

Project Implicit

Want to know more about implicit knowledge? In 1998 three scientists from the University of Washington, Harvard University, and the University of Virginia developed Project Implicit as a way to gather data on people's implicit biases. The tests are designed to measure reaction times when pairing certain images and words. The tests have two parts. For example, in the test designed to measure bias about women in the workplace, the first part has the participant match images of women with words related to the home and family, while images of men are matched with words related to career. In the second part of the test, the words are switched, so the work-related words are matched with the images of women and the home and family words are matched with the images of men. The participant is supposed to make the matches as quickly as possible, and the reaction time is measured and used to calculate how strongly the individual associates women with home and family or women with careers.

For more information on their project, you can visit www.projectimplicit.net. Or you can take a test yourself at www.implicit.harvard.edu/implicit/takeatest. While there is not currently a test to measure implicit views on sexual assault, there are several different tests measuring views on race, religion, and gender roles.[c]

being "no big deal." She proceeded, when she was nineteen, to be in an abusive relationship, an account of which is included next:

> The picture I had of abuse was so binary—it looked like a man literally punching his wife, my grandfather beating his children, or my great-grandfather molesting my mother. But those pictures are incomplete, and it's possible I kept those images in my mind so as not to break down as I grew up. Being a visual artist, everything to me had a picture, and the images I had of rape and familial abuse did not look like what I went through, so I chalked my experiences up as no big deal. . . .
>
> My first time having sex was forced—it was rape. I have a very hard time saying "rape" because it still does not fit my imagined view of rape,

which is violent and predatory, including screams and being pinned down. But it was rape.

I was fifteen, and was out at a hotel party on New Year's Eve, and somehow I had managed to get very drunk. I have no clue where the alcohol came from, but looking back I remember a lot of older men around who probably provided it—which is pretty scary itself. Even given what happened, things could have turned out far worse than they did.

I only remember pieces because I was so grossly intoxicated for the whole night. I remember making out with some guy in the stairwell, and the next thing I remember was being back in a room with my friends. I think it was their room but who knows. I don't remember how but the next memory is of being in a pitch black bathroom with a different guy trying to pull my tights down. I was pushed up onto a sink I kept falling from and he kept trying to push himself inside me. He tried and marginally succeeded, but he did so all the while hearing "no," or "ouch, it hurts" or some other resistance from me. He was not friendly or nice. He didn't try to kiss me tenderly, or be careful, because he didn't care. He started to get really angry because I kept expressing how painful what he was doing was, and because he couldn't get it in, so he said something like "fuck this" and pulled up his pants and left, slamming the door after him.

I was alone in the dark. I fumbled around trying to turn on the light, pull up my tights and walk out of the bathroom unashamed looking since there were a lot of people on the other side of the door. My thought process at the time was that I had failed at having sex properly. I pretended it was no big deal, and that it didn't matter. I didn't know who it was anyway, so whatever. . . .

To function, and not break down, I told myself again this was all no big deal. The problem with that is that you lose the ability to react to things that are big deals. At nineteen, I was in my second "relationship" although the guy didn't see it that way, to him we were just hanging out. It was full of verbal and emotional abuse, which of course hurt, but I didn't know what real love looked like, so to him (and all the others just like him who came later) I clung. After he had dumped me for not being his type, he called me back to go for drinks. I got really drunk, and we were on our way back to my place. He found a shortcut, over an eight foot fence. He got over easily—being a graf writer [graffiti artist] he was used to hopping fences. I got to the top, and though instinct had told me the whole thing was a bad idea, I still tried. I ended up falling eight feet to the ground and breaking my jaw, smashing a number of teeth, and fracturing my wrist. I think I had been unconscious as well. He would not take me to the hospital for fear of being blamed, and instead pressed me to smoke his weed to calm me down. I was again trying to tell myself that it was no big deal and that I would be ok in the morning. We got to my house where he tried to make out with me, and something finally broke the spell and I took myself to the hospital. The nurses were trying to contain themselves because I was a serious mess, which I tried to play down. I called him to tell him what happened, and he basically said he had to go and hung up on me. He had never actually put his hands on me, so how could it have been abuse?

None of this looked like abuse to me—in fact, on the outside, it looked like I abused myself. I got drunk, I stayed in these places that constantly hurt me, I never said no and created boundaries for myself. But I didn't know *how* to. It took me almost twenty years to understand this. I understand better that it can sometimes take a lifetime to change just one thing, and have begun forgiving myself for a lot of the things I felt responsible for when I was young. I'm not sure where the need to compare our suffering to others comes from. I feel it may come from our culture of domination that must have a winner in every situation, including in victimhood.

I have begun to try to recognize healthy dynamics between people, and dynamics of true human love between people—it is something I had to put a lot of work into, by looking inwards, asking for what I truly want or need and not feeling ashamed or too meek to ask for it. Not just romantic love, but all love, because I was lacking it in all areas, and I was unable to express it in all my relationships. I desire truly loving family and friendships to be a part of, to nurture, to honor. I have begun to try to treat my own body

Healthy relationships are built on mutual respect and good communication. It's important to learn how to communicate clearly about sex in a relationship.

with more respect, which simply means knowing my own boundaries and what is not acceptable. I don't want unsolicited sexual encounters, and I don't want to have sex with anyone where there is not a mutual agreement to look out for each other's well-being, as it has taken me a long time to realize how much our sexual encounters affect our whole lives, both men and women. I by no means have it all figured out. I am still learning. But that's ok, because if I am ever to have children, their starting points will be much more stable than mine, and to me this is what counts the most.[12]

The following story shows some of the pain and frustration that can be caused by abuse. While Monika was in a relationship with the boyfriend who raped her, other elements of this account resemble a date rape in that the rape was drug facilitated. Sexual assault and rape incidents often don't fit perfectly into a single category. Implicit beliefs about relationships and sex may have contributed to this sexual assault. Why would this boyfriend think that this was acceptable? Monika's story also illustrates the difficulty sexual assault victims who are in a relationship with the assailant have in identifying what has happened to them:

It was not the first time I slept over at his place. As normal partners, we cuddled, but we were in a relationship for one month, so I was far from ready to have any kind of intercourse with him. We didn't even talk about it yet. It was a beautiful summer night, we went to a party, with his friends. I was about to drink one beer, but he made me try his mixed drinks, which I didn't know what was in. When I was [turned] around, he (for fun) mixed something in my beer, his friends told me later. However, maybe he thought I was, but I was not even close to drunk to the point I would not know what I'm doing. He was more, but since he could drive home, he was obviously aware of everything, just maybe a little more "brave." We came home around 3 a.m. I changed my clothes and went to sleep. About five minutes of sleep, then he started putting his hands everywhere on my body. I turned to him, he took off my clothes, except underwear. I liked being cuddled by him and that was fine with me. Kissing, hugging, just lying with him and talking, I could be like that for hours. But then he wanted more. His hands started to focus mostly around "down-there," and he started making jokes of me, telling me what to do with his "tool." He tried convincing me, several times, then gave up. At that point I got scared. I didn't want to even touch it, and I told him clearly, no I don't want this, or any of it from this point on. He said, okay, and it seemed he understood, as he removed his hands and went back on just kissing and hugging. I was happy with that. Going on top of me, firstly just kissing all over my body, he was then about to take everything he wanted. We still were both partly dressed, but that didn't stop him. He didn't mind what I said before, however. In his mind, I probably should want it. When he started, I was so shocked, frozen, that I couldn't say anything, but was resisting him, as much as I could with him on top of me. But no, I wasn't one of those screaming, violent victims trying to get out of this. I was in shock. And frozen. I could barely move. Monika, wake up from this stupid nightmare . . . wake uuup! That's not real. That's not happening. No way, that can happen to me. "It doesn't go in," he said and almost gave up. But he didn't. In fact he was so persistent and violent, that he finally won. Although he did see I don't want it, he was making jokes of me, why I was so quiet, if I'm okay. There was no answer. He continued, but was smart enough to end up soon enough, not making me pregnant. Probably for his own good. He was aware of everything. That he wasn't so damn drunk . . . I was about to get dressed, when he asked me if I want to do it again. "I said no the first time" was my answer, shaking. If he thought before, this was romantic, at that point he probably knew it was wrong. I got dressed and told him to drive me home. He did. I knew I was not okay, needless to say I was in pain, but I was betrayed by the man I loved and trusted. However I didn't know it was legally wrong. At the same time, I hated and loved him. If that's possible. For three months, I was feeling totally down, thinking about suicide every day. In my mind, it was my fault. He just misunderstood the situation. I shouldn't have gone to his home. I shouldn't have got undressed. I shouldn't show him love. I should stop it, shouldn't freeze, shouldn't be in shock . . . how could he do this to me? He can't be so bad. I loved him, I can't be so wrong in my judgment. . . .

I never found out what he was thinking, did he know it was wrong or not.

It was five years later when I finally learned it was rape.[13]

How Are Subconscious Beliefs Developed?

Where do teens subconsciously learn sexually abusive and other abusive behaviors? There are several different places that people are exposed to these kinds of violent behavior. It could be from witnessing abuse at home or in the relationships of other teens. Even if a child's home isn't directly abusive or violent, the child may still be exposed to messages about abuse that make it seem acceptable. For example, when a little girl is being picked on by a boy, she is often told by a teacher or parent that the boy is only picking on her (or sometimes, hitting her) because he likes her. This sends the message that violent, abusive behavior is an expression of love.

Teens can also learn this mind-set from popular music, books, and movies. Sexual assault and sexual coercion in relationships are regularly trivialized in media, giving the impression that these are normal ways to show love in a relationship. Songs like Maroon 5's "One More Night" give the impression that not only are abusive relationships normal, but they are in some way more romantic. This is seen in other songs too, like in Pink's "Please Don't Leave Me," in which even though it's clear that the relationship is unhealthy, the singer prefers that to the idea of being alone. This theme is taken even further in Kelly Clarkson's song "My Life Would Suck without You," in which the relationship is clearly labeled as "dysfunctional," but it's made clear that the singer finds an emotionally abusive relationship preferable to being alone.

These kinds of messages about abuse are constantly present, and are constantly being internalized, creating implicit knowledge about what love is supposed to look like. Characteristics like jealousy, possessiveness, verbal abuse, and

Teen Dating Violence in the Twilight Saga

The four books in Stephenie Meyer's Twilight Saga, and the five movies based on them, have saturated American culture. A lot of Christian groups have praised the books for their message of abstinence before marriage. But does that mean that the relationships in the books are healthy?

The books contain several elements of dating violence in the relationship between Edward and Bella, and in the relationship between Jacob and Bella. But these instances of violence and abuse are trivialized and made to seem normal. Or they are romanticized and treated like signs of love.

For example, in *Twilight*, the first book, when Bella learns that Edward had been spying on her, instead of finding it disturbing she's flattered by it.[d] In the third book, *Eclipse*, Jacob kisses Bella against her will, and she breaks her hand punching him. Instead of this encounter being viewed as something negative, it's laughed about by both Jacob and Bella's father, Charlie.[e] An in-depth study of the Twilight books points out five cases of sexual violence, with Bella as victim in all five cases. Although Bella and Edward wait to have sex until after marriage, when they do have sex it is violent enough to leave bruises on Bella. The violence of the encounter is played down by Bella.[f]

There are thirty cases of physically controlling behavior in the series, twenty-eight of which involve Edward or Jacob controlling Bella. There are thirty-one times in the books in which Edward orders Bella to do something. There are sixty references to suicide or self-harm, two thirds of which are thoughts or behaviors of Bella. There are fourteen stalking instances, eleven of them with Edward stalking Bella. Also of note are the 183 instances of male aggression and male superiority, most of which involve Edward or Jacob.[9] The scary thing? Most of these actions are seen as being romantic, with millions of teenage girls rooting for Team Edward or Team Jacob.

To most readers and moviegoers, the more problematic messages from the relationships in the Twilight series may not be noticed. The books were international best sellers, and all five movies were blockbuster hits. The sheer popularity of Twilight seems to speak to the acceptance by teens and adults that possessiveness, controlling behaviors, stalking, and violence are all signs of true love. The romanticizing of dating violence in Twilight is both accepted because of implicit beliefs and adds to the canon of pop culture that builds implicit belief systems about what relationships and dating should be like.

in some cases even physical abuse are made to seem romantic and desirable. In this way, implicit beliefs about abuse and relationships not only contribute to an individual being abusive, but they also contribute to why someone may accept abusive behavior from the person he or she is dating.

Ending the Abuse: Getting Out, Getting Help

Teen dating violence, in all its forms, can cause serious problems for the victim, especially if he or she doesn't get help. Studies have found that victims who haven't gotten help are more likely to abuse alcohol and drugs, suffer from depression, and have suicidal thoughts or actions.[14] Victims of cyber-abuse are even more likely to experience depression and other issues as a result of the abuse.[15]

If you are in an abusive relationship, as the victim of abuse or as the perpetrator, it's important to end the abuse and get help. It is never too late to seek help and support.

How Outside Sources Provide Help

Depending on the kind and severity of abuse, getting help may mean ending the relationship. It may also mean seeking support from friends, parents or guardians, school officials, or professional counseling. In some cases, this may mean going to the police or to the hospital.

Friends can provide emotional support and help with the healing process. Friends are usually the first place teens turn to for comfort and advice. It's a good place to start. However, sometimes, more help is needed. It's good to be aware of other resources that are available, whether you need to use them yourself or encourage a friend to use them.

Parents or guardians can also provide emotional support. Even though it's sometimes hard to talk about sexual assault or other forms of dating abuse with them, parents can find ways to ensure your safety, especially after a breakup. They can also assist you in getting additional help if you need it. If you find that you have abusive tendencies, parents can also arrange counseling services to help you overcome these problems. However, if your parents or guardians are also abusive, if domestic violence is a problem in your home, it might be better to seek help elsewhere.

School officials, teachers, and guidance counselors can help in a variety of ways as well. They can rearrange your class schedule to help you avoid an abusive ex. They can create a record of the abuse, which you may need later. They can watch out for additional problems and make school a safer environment for you and others. They can also provide you with additional resources and information.

Split by Swati Avasthi

In Swati Avasthi's novel *Split*, sixteen-year-old Jace has run away from his abusive father and is staying with his older brother, Christian, who had left home many years earlier. *Split* closely examines the aftermath of violence at home and the many nuanced ways that such violence impacts all aspects of a survivor's life. It is also the story of overcoming, and of both Jace and Christian not letting the abuse of the past define who they are or what their future may be. In *Split*, Jace and Christian each get help from several informal sources, most notably from Christian's girlfriend, who plays a pivotal role in helping the brothers overcome their abusive past.[h]

Professional counseling can help the healing process go faster and smoother. It can help you understand the feelings and emotions that are caused by sexual assault from an intimate partner. Counselors can help you identify ways to create healthy behavior patterns and develop healthy relationships, whether you are the victim of an abusive relationship or the abuser. There are programs and counseling available

Breakup Tips

Breaking up is hard to do, and when you're leaving a violent relationship it can be scary. Here are some tips to break up safely:

- Build a support system of close friends and family.
- Let others know if you feel you may be in danger.
- Change passwords to email accounts and social media networks if your partner has that info.
- Avoid check-ins on Facebook or with apps like Foursquare. If it's an ugly breakup, it's probably best not to publicize your whereabouts. Ask friends not to tag you when posting location info as well.
- Adjust privacy settings and block your ex. Be aware that things you post on friends' pages may be visible to your ex, so be careful when posting on the pages of others.
- You can also deactivate your Facebook page when you log out so that no one can post on your wall or tag you in a post while you are logged off.
- Deleting your Facebook account all together is another option. You can always create a new one later.
- If you need to avoid seeing your ex at school, consider talking to the school guidance counselor or principal about changing your schedule.
- Ask friends to walk with you between classes to act as a buffer.
- Remember to create records of abusive behavior.
- If your ex doesn't accept that you are breaking up with him or her, simply stop accepting calls and replying to texts.
- Report any stalking or dangerous behavior.

for those who have a tendency to abuse others. It's important to get help early so that future relationships can be healthy and happy.

Police officers also create records of abuse. Your local police department would also be the place to press charges or initiate legal action against someone who has assaulted you. Often sexual assault, especially sexual assault from a partner, goes unreported. When deciding whether to file a police report, it's important to keep in mind that the person who hurt you will most likely go on to hurt others.

Hospital nurses and doctors create a record of the abuse as well. They also treat injuries that can be the result of dating violence. If the rape occurred within twenty-four hours and the victim hasn't washed or douched, doctors or nurses at the hospital can also use a rape kit to gather evidence. Sometimes evidence can be collected as late as seventy-two hours after a rape, but it's best to have a rape kit performed as soon as possible. Most hospitals are also trained and equipped to provide immediate counseling to victims.

It's important to document instances of sexual assault and abuse, even if it's just writing it in a journal or saving abusive texts or emails. If there is a documented history of abuse, then if things become more dangerous or threatening it will be easier and faster to get help. When you can show a police officer a history of violence and abuse, the officer will then be able to treat imminent threats more seriously.

Online Organizations for Teens Experiencing Dating Violence

Break the Cycle: Empowering Youth to End Domestic Violence: www.breakthe cycle.org

Love is Respect: www.loveisrespect.org

The National Center for Victims of Crime: www.victimsofcrime.org

The National Domestic Violence Hotline: www.thehotline.org

National Sexual Assault Online Hotline: www.online.rainn.org

No More: Together We Can End Domestic Violence and Sexual Assault: www .nomore.org

Online Organizations for LGBTQ Teens Experiencing Dating Violence

GLBT National Help Center: www.glnh.org

The Northwest Network: www.nwnetwork.org

The Trevor Project: www.thetrevorproject.org

SEXUAL ASSAULT OF CHILDREN

··

Sexual assault or sexual abuse of a child occurs when a person exposes the child to sexual acts or behaviors. It can include penetration; touching a child's breasts or genitals; making the child touch someone else's breasts or genitals; voyeurism, or looking at the child's naked body; exhibitionism, or the perpetrator showing the child his or her naked body; exposing the child to pornography; or using the child in the production of pornography. It also includes Internet abuse, such as distributing images of a child or contacting children online in order to groom them to engage in sexual acts.[1]

Incest is sexual contact between family members. It can occur between a parent and a child or between another adult relative and a child, but it can also occur between siblings. There are not hard and fast statistics for incest abuse because so many cases of incest go unreported.

Why would an incest victim not report? Because this is occurring within the family, the victim may care and even love the person who is being abusive. The victim may also feel guilt or shame about what is happening. The abuser could also be threatening the victim. Or the victim may believe that this is something normal that happens in all families. With most child sexual abuse, the person who is harming the child will often groom the child, and tell him or her things to increase feelings of guilt or responsibility for the sexual assault.[2]

Occasionally the media will report on a sensational story of incest that involves prolonged captivity or extreme circumstances, such as the 2008 Fritzl case in which a daughter was held captive in a basement by her father, who continuously raped her for twenty-four years before being discovered; the daughter gave birth seven times during her imprisonment.[3] It's important to remember that not all victims share that experience, that many of them live seemingly normal lives. That does not make their abuse any less real.[4]

The following story is from a man who was sexually abused by his stepfather for several years. Some of the physical symptoms he had as a child, such as the prolonged bed wetting, are actually symptoms often experienced by victims of

Child Protective Services in the United States

Throughout the early history of the United States, extreme cases of child abuse were occasionally prosecuted in courts of law. However, there were no agencies or reporting procedures or any laws pertaining exclusively to child welfare.

In 1874, the rescue of nine-year-old Mary Ellen from an abusive home in Hell's Kitchen inspired the creation of the New York Society for the Prevention of Cruelty to Children (SPCC). This was the first organized effort focused on child abuse, and it motivated similar charitable organizations to be created throughout the nation. The number of SPCC organizations peeked around 1922, at which point there were around three hundred such charitable groups throughout the country. However, this number was still vastly unqualified to handle all cases, and large pockets of the country had no access to such agencies.

In the early part of the twentieth century there were some minor efforts to begin the establishment of government agencies to address child abuse. It wasn't until the Great Depression of the 1930s, however, that responsibility for the care and prevention of child abuse began to shift from individual charitable organizations to state agencies. The first reason for this shift was that the steady stream of charitable donations that kept SPCC groups in business dried up during the Great Depression, causing many such organizations to close their doors or to merge with other charities. The second reason is connected to President Franklin Roosevelt's New Deal. As part of the New Deal, Congress passed the Social Security Act of 1935. A small part of the Social Security Act authorized the Children's Bureau to help state welfare agencies create and expand child protective services.

However, state agencies were slow to establish child protective services to replace the charitable organizations that continued to decline. For several decades, there were very few services available to abused children. Part of this was a lack of public awareness, including a lack of awareness and training among physicians. At this time, there were no reporting procedures for physicians to follow and no mandatory reporting required. So even if a doctor recognized signs of child abuse or neglect, there were no actions that the doctor might take to protect the child.

In 1962, pediatrician Henry Kempe published the ground-breaking paper "The Battered Child Syndrome." This article didn't just raise awareness among physicians; it also brought child abuse to the attention of the media, raising public awareness. The same year also brought the renewal of the Social Security Act, with an amendment requiring states to make child welfare services available statewide by July 1975. That same year, Dr. Kempe attended meetings held by the federal Children's Bureau to discuss ways to improve care for abused children. This led to the first mandatory reporting laws in 1963. By 1967, all states had laws requiring doctors to report suspected abuse and neglect.

Understanding and focus on the issue of child sexual abuse took longer to develop. In some ways, talking about child sexual abuse is still taboo. While newspapers and magazines in the mid-twentieth century were eager to publish sensational stories of children being beaten to death or severely neglected, they were not as willing to publicize stories of sexual abuse and incest. To an extent, even today such discussions are few and far between.

In 1974 the Child Abuse Prevention and Treatment Act (CAPTA) was passed. The law provided the first set of clear definitions of child sexual abuse. With CAPTA came the creation of a new government organization, the National Center on Child Abuse and Neglect. CAPTA provides states with funding to implement and run child welfare organizations, and puts a special emphasis on reporting and improved investigation practices. CAPTA was last reauthorized in 2010.[a]

child sexual abuse. This story also illustrates some of the manipulative behaviors the abuser will use on young victims:

First to start, I wet the bed, till about when I was fifteen. I don't actually know what happened that it stopped. I'm very ashamed of this. Until I was thirteen I didn't know I had this physical disorder that I had. I'd get leg cramps and such and cry in my sleep. It's important to say that I was crying in my sleep. I avoided crying as much as someone so young could. If I had cried while awake I'd very well have needed a reason to cry or I

Because of the secretive nature of incest, it often stays hidden in seemingly normal-looking families.

would have been given a reason that would make anyone cry. Somehow crying in my sleep soothed the savage heart of my stepdad. I suppose I couldn't be accused of doing that on purpose. Even wetting the bed didn't get the general reaction that it would usually. I would generally be given a very good reason to cry if I had wet the bed when I woke in the morning. He would wake me up very gently. He would help me clean up and change. He would then massage my legs with alcohol. After I calmed down and quit crying, he'd eventually start touching me in a not very good place for adults to do so. It really all started out very innocent until that started, then it started and really progressed fast.

It progressed from him touching me there to him having me do that to him. Then came my mouth. And then he started putting fingers inside me. This progressed to him putting his part there too. All very carefully. I did not really like it and it did hurt but he could hurt me worse. He was also much nicer during this than he would usually be. He said he loved me. Explained that was what this was all about. A convoluted set of words that made sense so young. I never knew to tell. Really never knew I could. There was no one to tell and I thought they knew anyway. This all lasted until maybe seven. Then he was out of my life mostly from then on. . . .

I started praying every night somewhere in there to wake up female. I saw how my sister was treated and I just thought I might be loved if I was a girl. In time until now I've been bulimic, a self-injurer, and just a lot of things I regret. It wasn't until twenty or so that I hit rock bottom. I just never realized in all my pain that I was loved. After attempting suicide, I found out that I was. I try hard to hold on to that truth. Life is not perfect but I've learned to accept those happy moments and try to keep them in my heart. I have fought not to get lost in the drugs that they did, and not to be this rage monster he was.[5]

Between Parents and Children

When a parent violates a child's trust by turning the relationship into something sexual, he or she breaks down a fundamental boundary. Because the child is dependent on and loves the parent in spite of the violation, the child will experience

Such a Pretty Girl by Laura Wiess

Meredith was supposed to be safe. Her father was supposed to stay in prison for molesting and raping her until she was eighteen, at which time she'd be free to move away.

But her father is released from prison three years early, when Meredith is only fifteen. And Meredith's mother is excited to have the family back together again.

Dark and disturbing, this work gives detailed descriptions of the aftermath from child sexual abuse.[b]

very confusing and conflicting emotions.[6] The child may even feel that he or she is to blame for the abuse and may feel shame that the abuse is taking place.[7]

Studies have found that victims of parent-child incest suffer greatly from depression. They will usually have more sexual partners both before and after reaching adulthood, and they are also more likely to cheat on their partners.[8] They are also often reluctant to talk about their abuse. This is possibly due to the fact that when they do open up about their abuse they are often met with shock or horror from the person they are telling. This reinforces the shame and the feeling of being damaged that they are already feeling. Because of this, survivors of parent-child incest rarely confide in their romantic partners.[9]

Usually when parent-child incest is discovered, the family unit is dissolved, with either the abusive parent leaving the home or the victim leaving the home. In spite of this intervention to stop the abuse, the victim of incest may still suffer from self-blame. For this reason, many therapists have what is called a clarification session to help the victim begin healing. In a clarification session, the abusive parent tells the child that the abuse was all the fault of the parent, not the fault of the child at all. This session can take place face to face, or if that's not possible, it can be done through a letter.[10]

The following story highlights several aspects of parent-child abuse. Although eighteen-year-old Peter is adopted, the circumstances of the abuse are the same as what is seen in other cases of parent-child abuse. This story also shows the disturbing ease with which incest abusers are able to go through the legal system, be convicted, and still not serve jail time. Additionally, Peter's story addresses the aftermath of abuse and the recovery process, topics which will be discussed at length in later chapters:

My story starts at age two. I was adopted from Ukraine. The day I was adopted was the day when the abuse started. My adopted father took me into a bathroom and sexually abused me. From that moment on I was abused regularly till I was eleven years old. I was abused alongside of my non-biological sister who was also adopted from the same orphanage as me. My father would regularly give us what he called "tummy rubs." These rubs would move from an innocent thing to the abuse. My sister and I were frequently abused at the same time, though we were both abused alone at times. When the abuse did finally come to light it was actually my sister who took it to my adopted mom. I quickly joined her in this attempt to bring the abuse to light, though I was not believed at first. My mom thought I was just bandwagoning for attention. I was eventually believed and my father decided to turn himself in to the police. He was arrested on one count of sexual battery but then given bail. After he appeared in court he was given probation and charged on the National Sexual Offender Registry. A restraining order was implemented and my mom started going through the divorce process.

This affected me greatly. I started being afraid of father figures and was very sensitive with anything stomach level or below. I also started making accusations in my head whenever I saw a dad with his kids. I would automatically assume that the dad was abusive and should be punished. I did suffer from nightmares. Furthermore if my stomach was touched even by accident I would have horrible memories and would feel angry towards who ever touched me. I was signed up for therapy with many different therapists but I was turned away after a few appointments saying my case was too bad. When I finally moved out to Utah I was suffering from depression and anxiety. I threatened to commit suicide. I was then admitted into a hospital. After about two days we started looking for residential treatment programs. I was able to find a residential treatment center that helped my overcome some of the struggles related to the abuse.

This healing process has been very hard. But through the help I received I was able to learn that I don't need to feel the need to say "it's okay" when my father apologized. I also learned that there was nothing I could have done and that the abuse was not my fault. Currently I am working on forgiving my father. Though I also learned that forgiveness doesn't mean accepting the crime.

If there was only one thing I would want to say to other survivors of sexual abuse I would tell them that it is not our fault as victims. We consistently blame ourselves for not fighting back or stopping the abuse. But we are not at fault. Whoever abused you is the person to blame. You do not need to be acceptant of what happened. It is totally normal to feel angry and disgusted towards the abuser. Just remember that we are strong as survivors. We can overcome this.[11]

It is also of note that in spite of the turmoil that Peter has gone through, and the rough road of recovery, he was recently awarded his Eagle Scout Award from Boy Scouts of America.

Between Siblings

It is believed that sibling abuse is the most common form of domestic violence.[12] Included in sibling abuse is sibling sexual assault, or sibling incest. Sibling incest has been defined as touching or fondling, masturbation, exposure to pornography, anal or oral sex, digital (finger) penetration, or actual intercourse. It can occur between a brother and a sister or between two siblings of the same gender.[13] Traditionally it's been believed that sibling abuse and sexual assault is most commonly an older brother assaulting a younger sister, however a recent study found that girls are as likely to be the perpetrators as boys, and also that boys are victimized as often as girls.[14]

Sometimes parent-child incest victims may in turn abuse a sibling.[15] It is also believed that children may engage in sibling incest in a misguided attempt to nurture each other when their family is particularly violent.[16] Often the abuse will continue for years, not ending until the abusive sibling moves away. In these situations, the abuse is reported only rarely. The abuser may threaten the victim, threaten other family members or pets, or offer treats or rewards in exchange for sexual favors.[17]

The following story is from Danny, a survivor who was sexually abused by his older half-brother:

> The only time that I remember was when Carlos had me in his bedroom, and forced me to suck his dick. . . . Thinking of how it looked and smelled grosses me out to this day! My sisters do recall there were times that they would hear me screaming and crying in Carlos's room, and he choked them and threatened he'd kill them if they said anything. That absolutely leads me to believe it happened more than I remember. I think I completely forgot the moment after it happened, and didn't know it had deeply affected me until I was about fifteen years old. When I looked back and realized what it was that I experienced, I was too ashamed to say a word. No one knew until I was twenty-three what had actually happened, and my sister completely believed it (she was the only person I told at the time), cause the exact same thing happened to her. She was raped. And around that same age, I was introduced to porn by Carlos, while he was watching porn. . . .
>
> From when I actually realized what happened when I was fifteen, it was a cold, dark, fearful frame of mind to live in. I began to feel secluded from the world, given the idea that now I wasn't a "man" since I was raped. Less than. Weak. At fault. Gay. The state of depression that I lived in for most of my life has been in that world of false stories. Lots of coping, with pornography, sex, long-term relationships, pot, prescription pain meds, mental and physical self-abuse, avoidance, and cry bouts. Not until today (December 24, 2015) did I actually believe that I have PTSD, and I'm twenty-six (just a side note my current psychologist observed and dissected for me). What I can say up until that realization, that I suffered from deep depression and anxiety, and still manage it to this day.[18]

In a Town This Size

A series of survivors from child sexual abuse were interviewed for the 2011 documentary *In a Town This Size*. The survivors were all abused by a well-respected pediatrician in a small town in Oklahoma in the 1960s and 1970s. It explores the dangers and hazards of a serial pedophile. It also looks at how statutes of limitation have prevented prosecution or any legal action against this abusive doctor.[c]

Pedophiles

Pedophiles are people who are sexually attracted to children, and they often prey on children they are close to. They often groom their victims by giving them gifts, taking them on outings, and giving them extra attention. Pedophiles can also use manipulation and threats to ensure that their victims don't tell others about the abuse.[19]

Human Trafficking

Children are at high risk of being caught in the trap of human trafficking. In the United States, the average age that girls become victims of prostitution is twelve to fourteen, and the average age that boys become victims is eleven to thirteen. Each year, 325,000 children are at risk of becoming victims of commercial child sexual exploitation.[20]

Homeless youth are often the victims of sexual exploitation. Racial minorities and children/teens who identify as LGBTQ (lesbian, gay, bisexual, transgender, queer/questioning) are at a higher risk of experiencing homelessness, and are then more likely to be exploited.[21] It's unclear why racial minorities and LGBTQ youth are at a greater risk for homelessness, but many homeless children and teens have been victims of abuse, either physical or sexual.[22]

Children and teens are also targeted for sexual exploitation and trafficking through the Internet. This exploitation may start as solicitation, requests for in person meeting, or exposure to pornography.[23] Other predators will slowly seduce the victim. He or she may listen to the youth's problems and offer sympathy. The predator may share hobbies or interests with the youth and may offer gifts. Slowly the predator will introduce sexual exploitation into the conversation.[24]

Kathy, a survivor of childhood sexual abuse.

It's important to know that more than 90 percent of children who are victims of commercial sexual exploitation have also been victims of other forms of child sexual abuse.[25]

The following story from Kathy illustrates the lasting damage that can be caused by childhood sexual assault, especially when it is ignored by others:

Born and raised in Chicago, my ethnic background is Hispanic (Puerto Rican) American (Polish) . . . . [I have] one sister, Lou, who is ten and a half months older. . . . At the age of four my parents divorced, and my mother remarried a man named Phillip. He was someone she already knew. He owned an apartment building and they also both worked at the company making good money, adding to the income from the property. We lived comfortably, maybe that's what blinded my mom. One day we were at a family gathering and I went to the bathroom, when I opened the door my stepfather was in there. When I went to turn away he shut the door on me to watch him urinate. I was only four years old, and couldn't figure out why. As time passed he did several other things that then I knew, or should say felt, were wrong. My mom had gotten sick and needed surgery. As she stayed at the hospital we (Lou and I) went home with him. He made us sleep in his bed and naked as he fondled our bodies. He was an alcoholic and heavy smoker, so he reeked like a bum in an alleyway. As I laid there while he did all he wanted with me, I think I said "Where's mommy?" I looked at my sister, Lou, but neither of us could save each other. I love her dearly.

As we were growing we stayed at my dad's grandmother's house every other weekend. And one time we were there and it was time to go back home. We both sat on the couch and cried. I now was five years old. My dad asked, "Why are you crying?" and I said Phillip shows us his penis. And my sister nodded yes. He went crazy, called the police and they went to my mom's house and he was arrested. My sister and I were taken to the emergency room. I can remember that when we were being examined my mother yelling out, "They're kids, they don't know what they're saying." But still I was too young to have a voice. We were both taken away from her and went to live with my grandmother and aunt on my dad's side. She had three kids all young and we became the babysitters. I had it rough, rougher than my sister because I was angry. And my sister, well, just went with the flow. I resented everything and everybody. I got many, many beatings for the both of us, then just sat in silence and rocked till I fell asleep. I could remember just wanting to die at such a young age. After two years of my mom visiting we were able to go back home. And yes, Phillip was still there. After just a little time passed, he began to be himself again. A disgusting sick man. In the apartment we lived in, my mom's room was towards the front and ours at the very end. He was there every morning at the crack of dawn in front of our doorway masturbating for hours at a time, whispering our names. Then he would come in to put his hands under our blanket, then came penetration. I was at the age to speak, but scared at the same time from my prior experience when I was taken from my mom, and I had seen how happy my mom was, I didn't want to hurt her. But later on in years I realized she wasn't happy at all, it was about being comfortable, material more than anything. Time went on, several years with unbearable things he made us do, and what he did to us—me. I was forever getting beatings because of all the hate I built up inside for my mother and him. I believe in my heart that my mother always knew, but was too comfortable to care. At eleven years of age my stepfather punished me, which was nothing out of the ordinary. I sat in my room, I was so angry and full of rage, hate, and aggression. I told my sister, "I'm telling mom everything that he does to us." I finally became full of courage and called her to me. I sat her down and commenced to tell all he'd done. She stormed out of the room and called him from outside, it was a hot day. He came in and she said, "We need to talk." We sat at the kitchen table. I remember just like today. My mom at my right, Phillip across, and my sister at my left. She told Phillip everything, then asked him "is it true?" He looked at her and softly smirked and said to her in her face, "Yes, it's true, but they look for it." I could've killed him with my bare hands. My mom cried and of course I was relieved and couldn't cry, I had no more cry in me. She made a scene and talked about leaving but we never did. And she promised it would never happen again. Not true, it did till I was thirteen years old when she chose to move to Puerto Rico with him and gave us the choice to go or stay. Sad to say we chose to stay and be homeless than continue living in abuse. He's now gone forever . . . but not really. Because I now torture myself. I ran the streets, began using drugs, having sex, partying, whatever I can do to forget, and cover my wounds. At thirteen years old I tried to commit suicide, I just couldn't take it any more . . . was it the abandonment, or the sexual abuse? Well today I can say it was both. The dreams, thoughts, pictures, images, smells, everything drove me crazy. I thought that when I grew up I would either be gay or a rapist. And I hated kids younger than me. For many years I lived in my own mind. I spoke and answered as if there were two of me, good and evil. I suffered from severe depression, severe anxiety, paranoid schizophrenia, and dual personality. . . . And always thinking, why? Why me? What did I do for all this?

Living at the hospitals from age thirteen to twenty-eight from trying suicide eighteen times and being mentally unstable I grew comfortable there and felt safe. Comforting others to comfort myself, listening to others' life stories that were all different, but at the same time all the same in the end. Full of sorrow, thoughts, strengths, and beliefs. I grew little by little. I still attend counseling and take medication, but, thank God, just for anxiety. I have always liked poetry, now even more because I feel as I put the pen to paper I release all the toxins in my heart, mind, and soul, music because it's soothing and sharing with others how I overcame the evil within and the evil on the out. Yes, I still have dreams or nightmares, I just had one the other night, but I now know I can't be harmed anymore because I am here. I survived to tell you.[26]

Identical by Ellen Hopkins

Kaeleigh and Raeanne are sixteen-year-old identical twins. Their mother is a politician campaigning for US Congress, and their father is a district court judge. From the outside, the family looks perfect.

But on the inside, Kaeleigh is being sexually abused by her father, and has been for years. Both twins are experiencing psychological damage and are self-abusing. The novel examines the effects of sexual abuse on the victim, in this case Kaeleigh, and how a secret of abuse can harm everyone who knows about it, which in this story is Kaeleigh's sister, Raeanne.[d]

Cycle of Abuse

Often pedophiles and those who commit incest are victims themselves. The majority of them come from unstable families and have suffered physical or sexual abuse themselves. These perpetrators often report feeling rejected by one or both parents.[27]

How a Bystander Can Help

It's important to know and recognize the signs that a child may be a victim of sexual assault or abuse. These can include bodily signs, such as bed wetting, headaches, stomachaches, and sore genitals. There are also emotional signs, such as acting out, fear, mood changes, sadness, or refusing to be alone with certain people. The child victim may also act in a sexual way with other children or objects. The child may also talk about sex and have knowledge of sexual acts that are not age appropriate. Signs of abuse are not always present, and the child may try to hide the abuse out of fear or love for the person who is abusing them.[28]

There are also warning signs that a person may be sexually assaulting or abusing a child. The person may show extreme interest in a child or in a particular age or gender of children. He or she may try to be alone with children and may spend more time with children than with other adults. He or she may be overly affectionate with a child and may insist on hugging, kissing, tickling, or wrestling with the child even when the child wants him or her to stop. The person may also discuss inappropriate topics with the child.[29]

Boy Scouts of America and Child Sexual Abuse

From 1965 to 1985, Boy Scouts of America (BSA) kept its own "perversion files," records of incidents of child sexual abuse occurring within the organization. In 2012, the Oregon Supreme Court ordered many of these records to be made public, bringing light to the fact that few of the alleged abuse cases were reported to the police.

In 2015, two years after the death of Connecticut scoutmaster Donald Dennis, seventeen men and two women came forward to file a lawsuit against the Boy Scout organization, stating that the BSA should have done more to protect the victims, who were abused by Dennis in the 1960s and 1970s.

Today the BSA requires all volunteers to complete training on signs of child sexual abuse, and use a system that prevents any Scout leader from ever being alone with a child.[e]

If you suspect that a child you know is the victim of sexual assault or sexual abuse, it's important that you report it. You can call the police or child protective services to report suspected abuse. Your report will be anonymous, and you could be protecting the child from ongoing abuse.

The following story is from Jannina, a twenty-three-year-old who was sexually abused by her half-brother. She disclosed the abuse to her cousin, who then told her aunt. Often children who are being sexually abused will disclose to a close friend before disclosing to an adult or authority figure, so it is important to educate children on who to tell if they know someone is being abused. Even though the aunt did not report the abuse to the police, this is still an example of bystander intervention. For Jannina, telling her cousin led to the end of her abuse, although not to healing. The damage from the abuse continued to cause harm in her life for many years:

I was eight years old when I learned that I had an older half-brother who lived in Colombia. He was seventeen.

My parents told me he was moving to the United States to come live with us. I was so excited. Every diary entry became about what my brother

Like a house built on an unstable foundation, abuse during a child's formative years can cause immense damage. But healing is possible, often with the help of counselors who are trained to work with trauma victims.

would look like, what he would think about me, all the things we'd do together, and about how I couldn't wait to meet him.

When the big day came, I'd love to say that things went great and we became best friends and all my dreams came true, but that just isn't the case. That just isn't my story.

Truth is, he really didn't like me at all. He preferred my younger sister and we fought a lot. I worshiped him and tried everything I could to get him to like me, but nothing ever seemed to work. We had rare times of peace in which I remember him teaching me some soccer tricks, and telling me about life back home, but for the most part, we argued often and he would tell me he didn't love me.

A year later things changed. I'll never forget the night everything changed. I was nine.

We were driving home one night in the van. My parents were in the front and my sister, brother, and I were in the back. My sister sat to my left and my brother to my right. About thirty minutes away from home my brother fell asleep, or so I thought. But the interesting thing is, he fell asleep with his hand conveniently wedged between the seat and my butt with his palm upwards so he was grabbing me. For some reason I thought this was so silly. I remember whispering and giggling to my sister and pointing telling her how funny it was that he had fallen asleep that way. I stayed totally still the rest of the way home so I wouldn't wake him . . . .

When we got home he stopped me on the way to my room. He pushed me up against the living room wall and said, "What happened back there, I am sorry. You can't tell mom and dad, it won't happen again." . . . I was so confused, I didn't realize what he was talking about and when I finally did, I didn't know how to comprehend that he hadn't been asleep, he had meant to grab me . . . I had mixed emotions. I felt strange, I felt burdened with some dark secret but in a way, I kinda liked thinking my brother and I now had something that was ours, it was our secret.

So from that night on, every car ride, movie night, walk to the park, and any time alone would become repeats of that night when everything started. It wasn't as bad at first. He would hold me, touch me over my clothes and slowly, make me believe that this was his way of loving me, and that this is what love really was. This was probably the most damaging thing he ever did.

Over the next year things would get worse. Over the clothes became under the clothes as little by little my reality, my childhood innocence was robbed from me leaving only empty, confused, gaping wounds and strange sensations that I could not describe or understand.

And that's the way abuse works. He got into my mind, changed my idea of reality and left me thinking I needed him. When the abuse wasn't happening he'd just go back to being mean to me and cruel so that I would eventually long for the moments of twisted kindness that I grew to believe was love.

A year later, I had finally reached my breaking point and I finally spoke out to my cousin who was two years older than me and I told her everything that had been happening. I don't remember exactly why I told her, or what I expected her to tell me or do in response, but looking back now, I think it was my soul's way of finding its release, my own way of finding my voice.

She went home that night and told her mother, my aunt, who would return the next day claiming my cousin had left her textbook at our apartment. When she arrived she sat me in the living room, surrounded by her and my parents and told me that my cousin had told her what had happened and that now I had to tell my parents. I know now that she had meant only to help me, but in that moment I felt like I was sitting in the judgment seat. I felt like I had let my brother down, and our secret was out. I had done something terribly wrong and surely, now I would pay for it. As I fearfully, and embarrassingly tried, in my childhood words to describe what had been happening, tears began to flow down my parents' faces. Their faces and wails of torment and hurt were something I could not process as anything other than proof that I had done something wrong. That day would scar me for a really long time. This moment would place its stamp of "unworth" on my life, until I grew old enough to understand otherwise.

I remember finally finishing talking and running to my room to write a note saying, "I didn't mean to, they made me tell, please don't be mad. I love you." And pasting it on the front door for my brother to see when he got home from school. But my dad noticed and ripped it off saying I was not to speak to him and not to say anything to him. When he arrived home, my heart was breaking and all I thought I had, this amazing relationship with my brother, began to crumble at my feet.

Those next few days were a blur. My parents told me he would be moving out in two weeks to Colombia and that I'd never see him again. I was left with an empty hole, a space, a longing to be loved, to be cherished, to be admired, and I didn't even understand what any of that really meant. I was nine.

After he left, I never sought out therapy, and life at home resumed, as much as it could to normal, and we all fell into a state of denial and tried to forget it all by just not speaking about it. But its effects on me couldn't be silenced. I began to look for the same sort of "love" I had received from my brother, telling myself I'd just find the brother I'd never had. I got along well with the boys, and found myself falling captive in their hands at the first sign of being liked, or appreciated, or even noticed. At nine years old, there's only so much you can do in school, but my first kisses, and relationships would begin a rocky, confusing road from that age onward. The boys picked up quick that I was "easy" and I was passed along, naive, and willing through them all.[30]

Getting Help

If you are the victim of incest or of a pedophile, it's important that you reach out and get the help that you need. You can reach out for help from other adults that you trust, including your teacher, school guidance counselor, or your doctor. Any adult you trust and are comfortable talking with may be a source of aid. However, if you disclose to one person and that person doesn't provide assistance, keep seeking the help you need. You can also seek assistance from more formal reporting methods. This may include reporting the abuse to the police. There are also several agencies that you can reach out to for help and support.

Resources

The National Center for Victims of Crime: www.victimsofcrime.org
National Sexual Assault Online Hotline: www.online.rainn.org
National Sexual Assault Hotline: 1-800-656-HOPE
Darkness to Light: www.d2l.org

AFTER THE ASSAULT

Sexual assault victims experience a wide range of reactions or responses after the assault. Some of the physical reactions last only a few weeks while others, such as panic attacks, can linger for years. The psychological effects can also last for years.

Physical Effects of Sexual Assault

Some sexual assaults involve force, while others, such as drug-assisted rape or an assault in which the victim freezes, may involve only a little force or none at all. Force during a rape can cause bruising or bleeding in and around the vaginal or anal areas.[1]

Another effect of sexual assault is painful intercourse, sometimes called dyspareunia. Pelvic pain and longer and more painful menstrual cycles have also been attributed to rape. Survivors of sexual assault also experience a decrease in sexual interest.[2]

Sexual assault victims are also at risk for STIs (sexually transmitted infections) and STDs (sexually transmitted diseases). These include HIV, genital warts, syphilis, gonorrhea, chlamydia, and others. Most STIs and STDs are treatable with antibiotics. If you have been a victim of a sexual assault, it's important to get

> "I've been treated for depression for almost ten years now. I have nightmares and I struggle to stay present during sexual encounters. I get scared when it gets dark, I get terrified after any loud noise, I feel gross as soon as sex is brought up, I am easily offended on any topic that is even slightly related to sexuality. I have been seeing a therapist since the incident in the hotel room which has helped immensely, but the pain is still there and the memories will always be a part of me."—Taysa, age 24[a]

Are Teen Sexual Assault Victims Being Given Needed Medical Care?

A 2015 study suggests that teens may not be getting all the services they need when they go to an emergency room after a rape. The Centers for Disease Control recommends a long list of tests and treatments for sexual assault victims, but this study seems to suggest that clearer guidelines from the American Academy of Pediatrics are needed that address how teen victims should be cared for.

Sexual assault victims should

- be offered emergency contraception,
- be tested for venereal diseases,
- be tested for hepatitis B if unvaccinated,
- be tested for HIV and syphilis,
- be tested for pregnancy, and
- be treated with preventative antibiotics.[b]

tested for STIs and STDs. Health care providers may not test for these automatically. Your state's Crime Victim Compensation Program may cover some or all of the costs of being tested.[3]

Panic attacks are another physical reaction that can occur after the trauma of a sexual assault. A panic attack is a sudden, intense feeling of fear or discomfort that usually only lasts for a matter of minutes. Symptoms experienced during a panic attack can include a racing heart, sweating, numbness or a tingling sensation, chills, feeling hot, feeling dizzy, nausea, chest pain, the sensation of choking, feeling a shortness of breath or a choking sensation, and trembling or shaking. However not all of these symptoms will be experienced.[4]

Hyperarousal can occur as well, which puts the survivor into a state of fight or flight. Hyperarousal symptoms include a racing heart, sweating, upset stomach, irritability, impulsiveness, anger, and insomnia. Hyperarousal can last for minutes or for an extended amount of time. Victims may also have re-experiencing symptoms, like nightmares.[5]

Other physical effects of sexual assault include urinary infections, uterine fibroids or noncancerous tumors, and a risk of pregnancy.

Psychological Effects

There are many different ways that a major trauma like sexual assault can impact a person, and it's important to know that everyone reacts to trauma differently. Here are some of the major ways that the trauma of a sexual assault can impact an individual.

Triggers

A trigger is something that reminds the victim of the sexual assault and then triggers a psychological reaction. A trigger can cause a flashback or it can cause the person to dissociate, or separate from one's physical reality and emotional state. Mild dissociation could be feeling detached, while more extreme versions can cause serious mental health problems. Triggers can bring on fight-or-flight responses in which the victim may simply flee from the situation or lash out in anger. Triggers can also bring about spells of depression for the individual.

A trigger can be almost anything. It can be a place, like the place of the assault. It can be a person who looks like the assailant. It can even be a smell. Exposure to sexual content in a book or a movie can also be a trigger. Or even a nonsexual touch on an area the perpetrator touched can trigger a victim of sexual assault.[6]

Post-Traumatic Stress Disorder

Post-traumatic stress disorder, or PTSD, can affect people after a traumatic event like a sexual assault. Some people may have symptoms of PTSD immediately, and then have those symptoms go away after a few weeks. This is called acute stress disorder, or ASD. When the symptoms are ongoing then it might indicate PTSD. Sometimes symptoms of PTSD may not occur for weeks or even months.[7]

There are four major types of symptoms for PTSD: intrusive symptoms, persistent avoidance, negative alterations in cognitions and mood, and marked alterations in reactivity. Intrusive symptoms can include involuntary and intrusive thoughts about the traumatic event. For children, this may include reenacting the trauma through play. Dissociative reactions, such as flashbacks, that force the individual to relive the experience are considered another intrusive symptom. Experiencing intense psychological distress caused by triggers is also an intrusive symptom. Persistent avoidance can include avoiding thoughts about the traumatic event, but can also include avoiding people, places, activities, or situations that resemble or are associated with the traumatic event. Negative alterations in cognition and mood can include the inability to remember specific or important details about the trauma and persistent negative beliefs about oneself or other people. A distorted understanding of the cause of the trauma, potentially leading the survivor to blame him- or herself, is also part of negative alterations in cognition as well. Marked alteration in reactivity can manifest itself as angry outbursts over small things, self-destructive behavior, being hypervigilant, sleep problems, difficulty concentrating, and an exaggerated startle response.[8]

For these symptoms to lead to a diagnosis of PTSD, they need to last for over a month; cause impairment to work, study, or relationships; and not be related to substance abuse, prescription medication, or another medical condition.[9]

In the following story, nineteen-year-old Toby shares some of the psychological impact from being raped, including some of the triggers that she lives with daily and her experience with PTSD:

> I was diagnosed with PTSD about four months after the assault, shortly after telling my family and receiving medical care. While I've learned to manage and cope with my PTSD, I'm keenly aware of its lingering presence on my life. To this day, I scream when someone unexpectedly touches me. I'm easily startled and become paranoid late at night if I'm by myself. There are triggers I have to avoid in my daily life, like the smell of Wintermint, which was the pungent scent I remember during my assault. His aftershave was Wintermint, and even the slightest whiff of it can lead to a PTSD episode/ flashback in which I feel as if I'm back in the scene of the assault again.
>
> While I believe more and more people are becoming understanding of PTSD, there's still a lot of confusion as to what other symptoms can be. Manifestations of my PTSD aren't always extreme, but rather can be things simple like social withdrawal. Sometimes, I won't want to be around people if only because the social stress is just too high. PTSD is a stress disorder, like the name says. There can be little stressors, like having to go to the doctor's office, knowing the "sexual history" section is going to be an obstacle. And there can be big stressors, like questioning why anyone would love someone who has been through something like this. Rapists don't rape to gain sexual pleasure. They rape to gain power. They rape because they know how to attack people when they are most vulnerable.
>
> It's difficult to be intimate with someone after an assault, despite how long ago it was. Rape was my first sexual encounter. I hadn't even had my first kiss when I was raped at the age of fifteen. Intimacy—both emotional and physical—has been difficult. Knowing that at any time during

what's supposed to be a loving encounter that you could have a flashback and experience a PTSD episode isn't fun. Instead of a loving experience, it can be a stressful experience. Rapists take away a person's dignity and self-worth. Robbers can take things that can be replaced. My watch can be replaced, my TV can too. My innocence can't. My virginity can't be replaced. My peace of mind cannot be replaced.

It's hard not to resent the body someone used and threw away.[10]

Children and teens can have different reactions to extreme trauma such as a sexual assault. In young children, common symptoms can include bed-wetting, forgetting or being unable to talk, reenacting the assault when playing with toys,

Should College Instructors Provide Trigger Warnings?

College is a time for learning and mental growth. Many courses, like literature classes, may contain material with descriptions that could be triggers for survivors of trauma. Some students have been pushing for professors to provide students with trigger warnings so that they know if required reading contains sensitive material, like depictions of sexual assault or extreme violence. Some instructors are also in favor of trigger warnings.

Proponents of trigger warnings point out that giving students trigger warnings does not necessarily excuse them from completing the required reading; however, because they know that the trigger is there, they can better manage their reaction to it. The students can take medication if that will help or ensure that they are reading the material in a safe, private environment.[c]

Others have argued that special treatment, like trigger warnings, gives students an unrealistic expectation to be protected from things they perceive to cause them discomfort. It's even been suggested that providing triggers that permit students to opt out of potentially offensive material could actually cause delays in the healing and recovery process.[d] It is clear, though, that as awareness about PTSD and other psychological difficulties that trauma survivors face grows, so will the number of conversations about triggering and trigger warnings.

or being unusually clingy or unwilling to leave a parent or other trusted adult. Teens may experience symptoms similar to adult symptoms, but may also experience behavioral problems, such as destructive behavior.[11]

Most rape survivors will develop some of the symptoms of PTSD following the assault. For about half of the survivors who experience this, the symptoms will go away on their own. For the other half symptoms will persist, interfering with daily life. Not only do rape survivors have extremely high rates of experiencing PTSD, but their PTSD symptoms may actually be more severe than what is seen in other types of trauma. Survivors are at an increased risk of being sexually assaulted a second time; for survivors who are re-victimized, the risk of PTSD is even higher.[12]

Self-Harm

Some individuals who have been sexually assaulted may turn to self-harm as a way to cope with the pain. Also referred to as self-injury or self-mutilation, self-harm usually consists of inflicting minor injuries on oneself as a way to create an outlet for some of the inner pain an individual may be feeling. Self-harm may include cutting, burning, biting, hitting, hair pulling, or scratching and picking at the skin. While most injuries are superficial, there is always the risk that the individual may hurt him- or herself more than intended or that an injury could become infected.[13]

For more on self-harm, please refer to *Self-Injury: The Ultimate Teen Guide* by Judy Dodge Cummings, It Happened to Me, number 46 (Lanham, MD: Rowman & Littlefield, 2015).

"I was diagnosed with severe PTSD about a month and a half after the attack. Another month after that I was diagnosed with Generalized Anxiety Disorder. I have panic attacks at least every other day. I get flashbacks constantly. I couldn't sleep for weeks because of them. While sometimes I put on a strong face, I struggle every day with my anxiety and depression because of this. I lost motivation to do anything. I am just now getting back on my feet, a whole year later. Sometimes I feel like that makes me weak but deep down I know that sometimes it takes even longer for some people. I am still alive and functioning and I am so proud of that. Now that I have survived this I know I can survive anything."—Meagan, age 18[e]

Traveling Challenges for Sexual Assault Victims

Because of the nature of trauma, there are a lot of everyday experiences that survivors of sexual assault can find challenging, including travel.

At the airport today, most passengers can simply walk through the scanner then move on to their gate, but the TSA has a policy of randomly stopping passengers after they have gone through the scanner to give them a pat down. For most passengers, this is annoying and somewhat invasive, but for those who have experienced trauma such as rape, having a stranger touch their bodies, even over clothing, can trigger strong emotional and physical responses, such as extreme fear or anger, or even a flashback or a PTSD symptom like hyperarousal.

Because of the need for airport security, it is unclear what can be done to protect sexual assault victims from invasive pat down procedures. Victims can inform TSA agents that they have experienced trauma and are sensitive to being touched. Passengers can also request the screening be performed in a private room and can request taking a companion with them. Pat downs are always performed by a TSA agent of the same gender as the passenger, and there should always be another TSA agent present during a pat down.[f]

Flashbacks

Flashbacks may be triggered by something in the environment or by a memory. A flashback can feel like the assault is happening again, as if the attacker is actually in the room. Flashbacks can happen at any time or at any place. Flashbacks can be an indicator of PTSD, or they can occur on their own.[14]

Depression

It's normal for those who have experienced sexual assault to go through a period of sadness or unhappiness. But if that sadness persists for weeks, and begins to interfere with daily activities, it could be a sign of depression.

"I had flashbacks of my sexual assault for years and didn't realize that's what they were. The word 'flashback' for me meant the scenes in movies in which war veterans are so immersed in the flashback's reality that they don't even know where they are. I had one flashback somewhat similar to that kind a few months after the assault. I was lying down while kissing my boyfriend and the flashback felt so physical, with the sense of touch as part of it, that it felt like a simultaneous reality with the present. However, most of my flashbacks were similar to intrusive thoughts—just, literally, a 'flash' of memory through my mind. Also in a similar vein to intrusive thoughts, the same snippet of memory would often repeat over a course of time—whether minutes, hours, or days."—Anonymous[9]

Depression is common following a sexual assault.

More severe forms of depression can cause the person to feel down or sad most of the time. The person may lose interest in favorite activities, experience weight loss or weight gain, have trouble sleeping, experience fatigue, have feelings of worthlessness or guilt, and have thoughts of death or suicide.[15]

There is no clear time line of how long after an assault feelings of sadness or depression may last. If you've experienced a sexual assault and are struggling to accomplish your daily routine, seek help. Depression is a mood disorder that in 2012 affected an estimated sixteen million people. It is a serious mental health illness. Counseling or other forms of therapy should be considered for treatment.[16]

For more on depression, please read *Depression: The Ultimate Teen Guide* by Tina Schwartz, It Happened to Me, number 42 (Lanham, MD: Rowman & Littlefield, 2014).

"Shattered"

The following poem, written by a survivor named Marissa, illustrates many of the damaging feelings experienced by survivors of sexual assault. A lot of the emotions described in this piece paint a vivid picture of what living with depression feels like. It also describes healing with help. Marissa includes a brief explanation after the poem about her experience:

Shattered

Crashing of the glass window shattering to the floor.
The sound is deafening and echoes in the interrupted silence.
Glass shards scatter, a million pieces never to be repaired, never to be
put back together.
That's how it feels.
When someone takes something away from you that you weren't willing
to give.
The person you once were, is no longer.
You're just like shattered glass.
Broken and sharp.
Just like the window, the light you once let shine through you is gone.
Numb, too scared to pick up the shards.

They're too sharp. The edges cut into you and so you leave it alone.

You even try to hide the mess and sweep the shards under a rug.

You even try to say to yourself that no one can tell you've been shattered.

And for a while, no one notices the broken window.

Then one day your memories, the shards of broken glass, the ones you've tried so hard to push down, all come back.

All of it comes rushing back like a flood.

Fast, and cold.

It could be a smell, a scent from long ago, that brings your mind right back to that moment.

Or a sound, a sound of a voice that makes your heart stop and your breath gasps.

And you go back to your mess. Your shattered mess.

The crash of the glass is more deafening now.

The broken shards break into more, sharper pieces.

And you try to show someone the mess.

You try to ask someone, anyone to help you.

Someone to help pick up the pieces of glass that are too sharp for you to hold alone.

And some will point fingers of blame and say that it's your fault that the glass shattered.

And some will pretend they don't see the pieces of glass, they don't see you're shattered.

And even more will leave you because they too can't handle the sharp edges of the cut glass.

They leave and it cuts you like a knife.

Cruel and deep.

You hate them all for leaving you a shattered mess.

For not helping you when you finally were brave enough to show them you had shattered.

But one day, someone does see you, and picks up a piece of glass.

"Let me help you."

You know you have to let them.

And they pick up the shards of glass, one by one.

And you both know it can never be put back together, not the same.

You're still broken.

You're still cracked.

You're still missing pieces.

But the shards of glass don't cut you like before.

The edges are dull.

The pieces slowly come back together like a puzzle.

And slowly, the light shines through again.

It's not as clear.

It's not as bright.

But it still shines.

And it will continue to shine, getting stronger each day.

You'll never be the same.

But the cracks and missing pieces make up an intricate window pane.

A beautiful, unique window that lets light shine through and dance on the walls.

You are not just a shattered mess.

You are not just a broken window.

You are a window with a different, but beautiful view.

That still lets light shine through.

Clear and bright.

I wrote this one night six years after I was sexually assaulted. I had recently dropped a glass bowl on the floor and the sound reminded me of when I was younger, the breaking of a window in my family's house. The noise frightened me then as it had now, but it also triggered other dark feelings often associated with my rape. I found that those feelings once simplified, was that the sound of breaking glass is tied to my memory of the assault, not because glass had actually broken in that moment, but because I could only articulate my feelings of what happened as being shattered. The word and the sound became tied to that memory and those feelings subconsciously by myself. The story is a stream of consciousness and the metaphor of the window breaking also represents the very long journey these past six years. The word "shattered" sounds like glass falling to pieces on the floor. The two adjectives that break up the story are there purposely to show the different stages and to bring back the quietness that is then interrupted by more words; like the silence that is interrupted by the shattering of glass. The ending, with the window pane, is something I hope I can attain in the future, as I am not there personally. Not yet. I'm still picking up the pieces. But I am learning there are positive outcomes in every situation. No matter how dark it may seem.

I hope that readers can relate but take solace in that they are not alone in their feelings. And I hope that articulating those feelings can eventually lead to healing.[h]

Substance Abuse

Those who are hurting emotionally from a sexual assault may turn to substance abuse as a way to feel better or to numb the pain. These survivors may be isolated and lack the support of friends and family. They may still be confused about the assault.

Some signs that substance use has become a problem include avoiding those who don't support the substance use, taking or borrowing money to support the substance use, driving when impaired, lying about the substance use, poor performance at school or work because of the substance use, and spending time with those who encourage substance abuse.[17]

For more on substance abuse, please read *Substance Abuse: The Ultimate Teen Guide* by Sheri Mabry Bestor, It Happened to Me, number 36 (Lanham, MD: Rowman & Littlefield, 2013).

Dissociation

One reaction that some people may have to trauma is dissociation. This is when a person disconnects from reality. There is a spectrum of dissociation, with the most mild form being similar to daydreaming and the most severe being a chronic disconnect that makes it difficult for an individual to function day to day.[18] This could be the mind's way to protect itself from traumatic thoughts, feelings, or memories.[19]

Dissociative identity disorder is what was previously called multiple personality disorder, and is an extreme form of dissociation. A health care professional is necessary to make a diagnosis.[20]

Jannina, age twenty-three, describes dissociation in the context of her other post-assault symptoms:

> After the event I began showing immediate signs of Post-Traumatic Stress Disorder. At the time I didn't know that's what it was and I didn't connect it with the rape. I started having extreme startle responses, I had nightmares, I had flashbacks of my childhood abuse, I developed an extreme fear of the dark and a fear of being alone with men. But one of the most severe and most noticeable signs was that I began to dissociate. Dissociation describes a wide range of experiences from a minor detachment from your immediate surroundings to a more severe detachment from physical and emotional experiences completely. You don't lose your sense of reality, but you detach from it. This became really clear when I was confronted. Whenever I was confronted I would shut down. Quite literally. I would roll up in fetal position, or stay completely frozen like a statue, and shut down. I would lose the ability to speak, to respond, to move, and would be stuck in this state for sometimes hours at a time. I learned later that it was my mind's way of preserving itself when I couldn't cope or couldn't deal with my emotions. I didn't connect this dissociation or any of these symptoms with the rape at first. I thought it must be from my childhood abuse, and I even blamed Evan [my boyfriend] originally for the dissociation, claiming it must be something he was doing wrong because I had never experienced that with anyone else before him. I grew angry, confused, frightened at the world and my healing took a turn for the worse.[21]

Eating Disorders

Some victims of sexual assault will develop an eating disorder as a way to cope with the stress and trauma of an assault. This may be a way to express overwhelming emotions or to exercise control when circumstances in life seem out of control.

Some common eating disorders are

- *anorexia nervosa:* this is characterized by self-starvation and extreme restriction of food intake. This can cause substantial weight loss and can jeopardize the overall health of an individual.

The psychological harm of a sexual assault can make connecting with friends difficult.

- *binge eating disorder:* this is characterized by excessive eating without re-gard to normal body indicators of being full—eating without control.
- *bulimia nervosa:* this disorder combines binge eating with purging, either through forced vomiting or through the use of a laxative.

Even though this type of unhealthy behavior may provide a temporary feeling of control or empowerment, the long-term effects can be extremely harmful.[22]

For more on eating disorders, please read *Eating Disorders*: *The Ultimate Teen Guide* by Jessica R. Greene, It Happened to Me, number 39 (Lanham, MD: Row-man & Littlefield, 2014).

Sleep Problems

There are many sleep problems that can affect the survivors of sexual assault. These include trouble falling asleep and difficulty staying asleep. Survivors may also experience nightmares, night terrors, or insomnia. Other issues that may oc-cur are sleeping too much or sleeping at unusual times during the day.[23]

"After the abuse, I didn't trust people like I used to. Connecting with others became difficult, especially family and friends. Before, I was very open and had great relationships. But after everything I'd been through, I withdrew from social activities and saw people less and less. I thought they'd hurt me too. I was a scared, anxious wreck. My circle of friends shrunk and my family's concern grew as I isolated myself from them. School wise, I scraped by in my college classes. I'd usually made A's and B's, but stopped doing well academically after the abuse. I managed to pass with C's and D's. But sometimes I'd fail, so I had to repeat a few classes. Also, my health declined. I stopped eating regularly; I slept all the time and got very sick. Overall, my mental and physical health spiraled drastically. I couldn't recognize myself anymore and felt like a shell of who I'd been."—Destiny[i]

With all of the psychological effects of sexual assault, it's important to remember that each survivor experiences these effects differently. Some may experience lots of different symptoms and problems, while others may only experience a few. Rarely do these symptoms or disorders occur in isolation; there is usually a unique combination of challenges that each survivor will face.

Resources

Sexual assault is both physically and psychologically traumatic, but there are resources for those who are suffering the aftermath of a sexual assault.

National Eating Disorder Association: 1-800-931-2237 or www.nationaleating disorders.org

National Sexual Assault Hotline: 1-800-656-4673 or chat online at www .online.rainn.org

National Suicide Prevention Lifeline: 1-800-273-8255

Self-injury Outreach and Support (SiOS): www.sioutreach.org

Substance Abuse and Mental Health Services Administration: www.find treatment.samhsa.gov

Substance Abuse Treatment Referral Helpline: 1-800-662-4357

The Trevor Project (for LGBTQ youth): 1-866-488-7386 or www.thetrevor project.org

6

BREAKING SILENCE

··

Telling someone about being sexually assaulted is extremely difficult. There is a lot of fear about how the person will react. Survivors of sexual assault often suffer alone because of this fear. It's also hard to know how to respond when someone confides in you about sexual assault. There are many different ways to disclose sexual assault. Some people choose to disclose through formal channels such as rape crisis centers, hospitals, and the police; this chapter will discuss all three in greater detail. Formal sources of help can also include counselors and therapists, religious leaders, and campus reporting personnel. Informal sources include friends, family members, and romantic partners.

That Time You Told
by Hayley

The sound produced in your larynx and uttered through the mouth. The range of pitch or tone with which you sing. Expression in words. An uttering with resonance of the vocal cords.
Voice.
Your voice.
Use it, they said. Don't be afraid. You are powerful and mighty, and this voice is your weapon. Tell all of your worries, your pain, your anger. Tell it. Use it. Don't be silent.
Because even when it happened, you were not silent.
Even through the pain, through the confusion, through the tears, you whimpered. It was small and caught in your throat, but audible nonetheless.
The complete absence of sound. That is what silence is.
You were not silent.
You are not silent.
Think about what you want to say—what you need to say. What happened, and how that made you feel; how you feel about it now.
Say it, write it, tell it.
Twelve years. Today marks twelve years since that whimper passed through your lips.

Eleven years and eleven months since you found your voice, and uttered
the story to someone you thought was a friend. It has been nine years
and seven months since you first wrote your story down. Since you first
penciled in courage, and questioned the burden of blame.
It took six years. Six years for you to write the story where the main
character isn't guilty, where she did nothing wrong.
Three years ago she saw something in herself. That character of yours,
she found hope. Hope in the reflection of her eyes as she looked at
herself in the mirror, half of a laugh squeaking out audibly into the
empty room around her.
Then, eight months ago you wrote the word *survive*. You wrote it and
you believed it. She is a survivor, that character of yours. Her story
keeps changing, progressing, growing, and no matter how many times
you send her to hell, she keeps coming back—fresh on the page, ready to
live it again, survive it again, find hope again.
Today marks twelve years since that whimper passed through your lips.
Today you do not misplace blame. You do not carry guilt, or question if
she deserved it—that character of yours, you. Twelve years you and her
survived, found hope.
For twelve years you were not silent.
You were not silent.
You are not silent.
Today you have your voice.
Use it, they said. Don't be afraid. You are powerful and mighty, and this
voice is your weapon. Tell all of your worries, your pain, your anger. Tell
it. Use it. Don't be silent.
Today, and every day, I have a voice.[1]

The decision to speak out about a sexual assault is a very personal one. Some people never disclose their assault. Others will tell a few people but not others. Some may file a police report and yet never tell family members. No one should make you disclose a sexual assault if you are not comfortable with the disclosure.

Often victims of sexual assault will not disclose the assault right away. Sexual assault is a very traumatic experience, and it can take a person time to process what has happened. Also, in cases of acquaintance rape or date rape, especially those that are facilitated by drugs or alcohol, it may take the victim time to even label what has happened as rape.[2] When a rape does not look like a stereotypical rape, when the perpetrator is known, when there is alcohol involved, victims may also fear that they won't be believed if they report the incident.[3]

The following story from Toby, age nineteen, illustrates how fear of not being believed can cause a survivor to delay telling others about the assault:

I was a month shy of sixteen years old when I was raped by my best friend. We were on a summer mission trip—he was the oldest, I the youngest. We'd gotten to be extremely close over the months we'd spent together. He'd become a brother to me. I was blindsided by what happened the last night of our trip when he said he wanted to talk. I had no reason not to trust him and every reason to believe everything he said. He was my big brother on the trip, the one always looking out for me. He used my trust and innocence against me, leading me into a dark room where he stole my virginity, innocence, and feeling of security. I fought back, but I was 5'1" and barely 100 pounds. My 6'1" 210-pound opponent overpowered me. It wasn't a fair fight, one evidenced by the concussion, broken rib, and bruises my body sustained. During the assault itself, I felt like I wasn't human. I felt like an outsider in my own body. The best way I can describe it is it felt like a bad dream, only this time when I "woke up" I was covered in bruises, tears, and blood.

It wasn't until a few months later that I told my family. My health had been declining and I'd barely spoken or eaten. I was dying on the inside with a secret that threatened to eat me alive. Sleep and I hadn't seen one another in months. The tears eventually stopped coming when I became numb to it all; only then did I realize I needed help. Telling my family what had happened was probably the most difficult thing I've ever had to do in my life. At the time, I felt like no one would believe me and that if they did, they'd say it was my fault. The man who raped me had told me during the assault that no one would believe me. I was ashamed of what I'd done and hated the body he'd so cruelly objectified. I convinced myself my once best friend was right—that no one would believe me. He was wrong. They believed me and supported me as best they could, if only I would've been strong enough to let them help me sooner.

My family believed me. The police were a bit more hesitant, as almost a year had passed before I finally felt comfortable enough to come forward. By coming forward, I came to terms with the reality that this wasn't my secret to keep—it was his.[4]

Deciding to Disclose

There are many other factors that may influence a person's decision to disclose sexual assault or not. Here are a few of them:

- *Age:* Younger victims are more likely to delay telling anyone about the assault, or to not tell at all.[5]

- *Race/ethnicity/culture:* Victims of color face many challenges when reporting incidences of sexual assault. One of them is the prevalence of rape myths that hypersexualize women of color. Authorities and others may not believe a black woman who is reporting a rape because of a belief that black women are always sexually available. There are many ways that race and culture impact the experiences of survivors when they are deciding if and to whom to disclose an incident of sexual assault.[6]

- *Gender:* Rape is often viewed as a woman's issue. When a man is reporting rape, he is often not taken seriously if the assailant is a woman. If the assailant is a man, then the victim's sexuality is called into question. Men are much less likely to disclose incidents of adult sexual assault than are women.[7]

- *Social class:* Poorer victims of crime, including victims of sexual assault, face additional questions as to their creditability by those in authority. When social class, race, and culture intersect, such as a poor Latina woman who may face language barriers, reporting a sexual assault or accessing services to help in the recovery from a sexual assault becomes even more challenging.[8]

- *Parental communication:* Some studies have shown that young women whose parents talk to them openly about sexual relationships and healthy

Glee Episode Discusses Sexual Assault

In an episode in season 4 of *Glee* that aired in April 2013, two characters, Ryder and Kitty, share experiences of being sexually assaulted. While much of popular culture supports rape myths and victim blaming, it is cause for hope when there's an example of addressing sexual assault in a popular series watched by thousands of teens. The first disclosure, that Ryder had been sexually molested by a female babysitter when he was eleven, is met with stereotypical rape-myth reactions, that the molestation must have been a "fantasy come true." While some emphasis is placed on the seriousness of sexual assault, there is still room for improvement. For example, it would have been desirable for *Glee* to challenge the rape myth that a young boy being molested by an older woman is not harmful, or that young boys and young men view the possibility of such an incident as a "fantasy." Kitty's disclosure is much more private; she shares her experience with Ryder alone.[a]

sexual behaviors are more likely to disclose to their parents and to others if they are sexually assaulted.

Formal Disclosure Sources: Reporting Assault

Sometimes people aren't sure if they should report a sexual assault. What if the rape was interrupted? What if you know the person who assaulted you? What if you are in a relationship with the perpetrator? What if there are no physical injuries? In all of these situations, it's still important to consider reporting the incident. The people who sexually assault are often serial criminals with multiple victims. By reporting what happened, you could be preventing future assaults.[9]

At the same time, there are many obstacles to securing justice through formal channels of reporting and prosecuting sexual assault. Very few rape cases actually go to trial, and of those, few lead to indictment. A survivor who is working on healing and recovering from a traumatic event needs to put self-care first. There is no guarantee that there will be justice.

If you have suffered an assault and do want to press charges, there are some things to keep in mind. There could be vital evidence on your body or clothing. It's important to seek medical help or police aid as soon as possible after a sexual assault, but that doesn't mean doing it alone. Sometimes a trusted friend or close family member can provide the emotional support needed to seek help.[10] An

The decision to disclose sexual assault is very difficult.

important place to go first when deciding whether to report a sexual assault is your local rape crisis center.

Rape Crisis Center

Most rape crisis centers provide short-term group or individual counseling to help start the healing process. They can also get you in touch with long-term therapists or counselors who are experienced in working with trauma and sexual assault victims.

Rape crisis centers also provide advocates to help you if you choose to report the sexual assault. A volunteer or advocate can accompany you to the hospital for a forensic exam and to the police station to file a formal report. A volunteer or advocate can even go with you to court if your case is being prosecuted. Some rape crisis centers can even provide you with legal counsel or a legal aid representative to go with you to court and assist you through the legal process.

Hospital Emergency Room

Going to the hospital after a sexual assault is very important. If you suffer any injuries from the assault, medical treatment may be needed. Also when you go to the hospital, you can get treated and tested for STDs and STIs (sexually transmitted diseases and infections), and you can get emergency contraception to prevent pregnancy.

DNA evidence needs to be collected within seventy-two hours of a sexual assault; however, other types of forensic evidence may be collected after this time frame. Before going to the hospital, you should avoid disturbing any of the evidence of the assault. Do not shower, bathe, or change clothes. Do not comb or brush your hair. Do not brush your teeth. Do not clean up the area where the assault took place. Try to avoid using the restroom. It's natural after a traumatic event to do these types of activities to restore a sense of normalcy, but doing so can destroy vital evidence. You can pack a change of clothes to take to the hospital with you.[11]

At the hospital trained nurses can gather forensic evidence by performing a sexual assault forensic exam using a rape kit. The kit usually contains a checklist, swabs, material for collecting blood, envelopes to seal the evidence in, a comb, documentation forms, and instructions.[12] Evidence will be collected from your clothing and from your body. The actual exam can take several hours. The exam will cover most of your body, including any areas that may have been penetrated by the perpetrator. Pictures may also be taken to document any injuries. You can contact your local rape crisis center and ask for an advocate to go with you to the hospital, or you can ask a friend or family member. However, if you ask someone other than the advocate to be present during the exam and you later report the crime, that person could be called as a witness.[13] Not all hospital personnel you encounter will be trained in how to treat someone who is suffering from a traumatic experience like sexual assault, so having an advocate with you can help.[14]

At this point you can report the crime, and the hospital can get you in touch with the police, or you can have the hospital file the rape kit as a Jane Doe rape kit, giving you an identification code so that you can press charges later if you decide to.[15] Become familiar with the laws in your state for how long forensic evidence will be held and how much time there is to file charges. The DNA evidence is an important part of filing charges, because even if the perpetrator isn't convicted, the DNA evidence may be submitted to the national database, making it easier to identify and prosecute if the same person commits another sexual assault.[16]

Reporting to the Police

When you report a sexual assault to the police, they will conduct an interview with you. It's important to know that during this interview you have a right to privacy. If you aren't being interviewed in a private setting, you can request more privacy. You can also have someone with you for support. If you don't have a friend or family member that you want present, many rape crisis centers have victim advocates

Outlawed in Pakistan

As challenging as it can be to report sexual assault in the United States, and as frustrating as it is not to be believed, the way that rape and violence against women are handled in other parts of the world is even worse.

The documentary *Outlawed in Pakistan* follows the story of Kainat Soomro and her struggle for justice. Kainat was gang-raped by four men in her village in 2007 when she was just thirteen. The village elders felt that, as a woman who had had sex outside of marriage, she should be put to death. Kainat's family had to move because of harassment and death threats. During a trial Kainat's assailants were found innocent. Kainat's brother was later killed in retribution for the family pressing charges. The film shows the continued persecution of the Soomro family for speaking out against rape.[b]

who can accompany you. The interview process may take a while, and you may hear the same question more than once or the same question worded a different way. This is because the police are trying to get specific details about the assault that will allow them to pursue a prosecution. If you are uncomfortable or are feeling tired or overwhelmed, you can ask to take a break.[17]

Sometimes the reactions that victims receive from the police are negative. Police may question a victim's story or ask questions that blame the victim. These types of negative reactions are sometimes referred to as secondary victimization, the second injury to victims, the second assault, or the second rape. These terms are used as a way to describe the harm and injury these types of negative reactions can cause victims of sexual assault.[18] Part of the reason that victims have negative experiences reporting to the police is that individual police officers may adhere to rape myths and victim blaming, including myths based on race, and this could affect the way they treat victims.[19] Another factor is that police are aware of how certain victims and circumstances will "look" if a case were to go to trial. District attorneys may not be willing to pursue cases in which the victim could be easily discredited or viewed in an unsympathetic light.[20]

The following story from Meagan, age eighteen, shows how she disclosed first to her therapist and then to many others. The only negative reactions she received were from the school and the school security officer:

> I was seventeen. The first person I told was my therapist who I had been seeing for several years because of previous depression issues. The next person I told was my mom and she told my dad. They asked a lot of uncomfortable questions, but they both believed me wholeheartedly. They then scheduled me an appointment right away with an OB/GYN so that I could get proper testing done. Luckily I wasn't pregnant but he did give me trichomoniasis which is a very common STD. I thank God every day that it was so easy to treat. It only took three months and then my tests came back clear. Most people who have this virus don't even know it. I still have no clue if he knew he gave it to me. After the doctor and the nurses the next person I told was my boyfriend who was just a really good friend at the time. He was super supportive and walked me to every class because for several months Steven stalked me from class to class. After I told my boyfriend I then told my school because Steven assaulted me there also by getting me into a back hallway and then he slammed me against a wall and kissed me as he pulled my hair. Luckily that was it and he left. The school did nothing, even after three other girls came out about him assaulting them also. The school ignored us and at one point the security officer called us all liars. That was the first time someone didn't believe me. It was hard because everyone could clearly see how violent he was. She

[the security officer] was clueless and it ate me up inside for a long time. In the past few months I have learned that I need to forgive her because she didn't know any better. After I finally told someone I felt empowered. Not broken like I had for a long time. It became addictive, it was like I wanted every single person to know my story and for a long time I had no clue why I felt that way. Now I realize it's because of all the other girls that came out about it because of me. He raped six other girls and molested and assaulted three others. Some as young as thirteen. He was and still is sick and I doubt he will ever stop. I have no clue where he is today, if he's now in college doing this to girls there or if he finally got locked up because he messed with the wrong girl. Someone who was strong enough to stand up for all of us. I hope that happens one day. I wish it could have been me that did that but I waited too long to tell anyone.[21]

Informal Disclosure Sources

A lot of victims of sexual assault will not seek help from formal sources, however; they are more likely to confide in a close friend than to seek professional help. This section provides information in case you are the one from whom a friend seeks support following a sexual assault.

Sometimes a good friend can offer a listening ear and emotional support.

Three forms of positive reactions to disclosure of sexual assault have been identified by researchers. They include emotional support, tangible aid, and information support.[22]

Emotional support: A positive reaction to the disclosure of a sexual assault includes letting the victim know you believe him or her, letting the victim tell the story in his or her own way, and offering the victim emotional support. Acknowledge that this has impacted the victim's life by simply saying "I'm sorry" or "I know this is really hard for you" and let the person know that this is not her fault. It's also important to let victims know that you believe them and that it doesn't change the way you see them. Offer continued support during the healing processes, remembering that everyone heals at his or her own pace.[23] If the victim is someone that you are in a romantic relationship with, emotional support can include letting him or her know that the physical aspect of that relationship can slow down or be on hold while he or she is recovering from the assault.[24]

The following story illustrates the emotional support that Jannina, age twenty-three, received from her boyfriend:

> The topics discussed in therapy must have brought up memories of the rape and I found myself beginning to remember it all. I didn't know what to do about it and after Evan proposed to me . . . and after I said yes, I found myself growing anxious about him not knowing. I was nervous about getting married and having him find out and not loving me anymore. I thought he'd be mad at me and that he would break off our relationship.
>
> A year later . . . I could carry the burden alone no longer. Crying, I brought him into my room and began to tell him what had happened to me three years ago. He cried and held me and we cried together for a long time. I sobbed apologies and he just hushed me and held me close. It was like I had finally let go of the burden. He knew, he still loved me, and everything would be ok. I felt a thousand pounds lighter and finally, I felt free.
>
> That was only four months ago, but already, I feel like a different woman. I already have seen the changes, not only in myself, but in my family.[25]

Tangible aid: This can include taking the time to visit with the survivor, or going with her or him to the hospital for medical care or a forensic exam. It can also include accompanying her or him to the police to report the crime.[26] While it's good to encourage a victim of sexual assault to tell others and to seek professional help, too much pressure to do so can actually harm the victim.[27] If the assailant is someone at school or on a college campus, tangible support can include walking with the victim to and from class to act as a buffer if the assailant were to try to initiate contact.

Canary by Rachele Alpine

Sometimes victims of sexual assault do not report the abuse because they fear what the consequences of speaking out could be.

In the book *Canary*, the main character, Kate, is a new student at an elite boarding school. Her father has just gotten a job at the school, and things are looking up. Kate seems to fit right in, quickly getting involved with the school's athletic department. Everything is going great—until Kate is raped by a friend.

Now she is struggling: if she says something, it could cost her father his job. But the effects of the assault are beginning to weigh on her.[c]

Information support: Providing a survivor with information and resources can be an important milestone in that person's healing/recovery process. Books, websites, and informative pamphlets are all great sources that you can refer a friend to.

Unfortunately, you may not know the best way to react to the disclosure of sexual assault. Some common negative reactions include asking questions that blame (like "Were you drinking?" or "What were you wearing?"), asking for specific details and causing the victim to relive the trauma, not believing the victim, or trying to force the victim to seek help from the police or at the hospital when the victim is not ready to do so.[28]

It can be hard to hear about sexual assault, especially from someone you are close to. Some negative reactions that survivors of sexual assault experience are caused by the relationship the person being told has to the survivor. These have been termed egocentric reactions. An example of an egocentric reaction would be the boyfriend of a rape victim getting angry and threatening to hurt the assailant. This reaction, though based on feelings of love and a desire to protect, does nothing to aid the victim and can actually cause the victim more stress.[29] Another egocentric response is when the person being told realizes that this is something that could happen to her. She may see the similarities between herself and the victim and want to distance herself from the victim. This leads to another negative reaction, which is victim blaming. The friend may ask the victim a series of questions that imply the victim is to blame for the assault. The friend does this not to hurt the victim, but to establish for herself that her personal choices would have been different, so this couldn't happen to her.

Another negative reaction is distraction, or avoidance. The person hearing about the assault doesn't know what to say or doesn't want to be involved, and may try to change the subject or end the conversation as soon as possible. This is harmful for the victim because it may stop her or him from seeking help from others.[30]

Stigmatizing victims, or treating them differently after a disclosure, is also harmful in that it can cause greater psychological problems for the victim. At the same time, minimizing the damage from the assault, or trying to make the victim feel that he or she is overacting to the trauma, is equally as damaging.[31]

In the following story, Taysa, age twenty-four, shares some of the reactions she has received and how she tries to protect herself from negative reactions. Taysa also includes the reaction she received from someone she was dating:

> After a few years I told a few people about the incident but would speak in a nonchalant way so that if the person I'm telling has an awful reaction, I'm able to brush it off and keep that "I don't care" attitude. That didn't mean that I didn't care. I remember the way I told one of my ex-boyfriends years after the assault. I remember the way it came out of my mouth and how far removed I felt when I was saying it. I've conditioned myself to pretend that something that really tears me apart inside doesn't, using jokes or laughter to mask it. I always hoped he (and anyone else I told) could read between the lines, see my pain and realize that it was a cry for help. Unfortunately he didn't take to the new information well. I tried for so long to convince myself that it didn't matter to me if he believed me or not, but ultimately I couldn't pretend that I was okay. I told him that I needed him to believe me and be on my side. I understood that he's a male and in that sense may not have a similar experience to relate to, but he's also not homosexual, destitute, or a drug addict and I know he's capable of empathizing with their experiences. I know it's harder because it's a sexual issue of mine and I was his girlfriend, but I needed his support. Unfortunately he was not able to get past the details of what had happened and we eventually broke up.[32]

Anonymous Disclosure Options

Victims of sexual assault may want to share their experiences, and hear from others who have had similar experiences, but are not ready or comfortable to disclose to formal sources, or to informal sources such as friends and families. For these survivors, online hotlines, chat rooms, and discussion boards may be appealing. Please exercise caution when using these services, especially if you are living in an abusive situation. A secure hotline is the National Sexual Assault Online Hotline at www.online.rainn.org.

Celebrities Breaking Silence

Sexual assault can happen to anyone, including celebrities. Many celebrities have spoken publicly about being sexually assaulted, either because the incident was public in nature or because they wanted to raise awareness about sexual assault. Here are some celebrities who have spoken out:

Maya Angelou: She was raped at the age of eight by her mother's boyfriend. Her first published book, *I Know Why the Caged Bird Sings*, is partially autobiographical and addresses both her rape and her teen pregnancy. Because of these topics, the book has been criticized by both parents and educators. Many of Maya Angelou's poems address topics of sexual assault and child abuse. Maya Angelou died at age eighty-six in 2014.[d]

Fiona Apple: Musician Fiona Apple was followed home from school one day when she was twelve years old. The man followed her into her building and raped her in the hall outside of her apartment. In an interview with *Rolling Stone* in 1998, Fiona expressed great fondness for the writings of Maya Angelou.[e]

Fantasia Barrino: She won the third season of *American Idol* in 2004 and went on to release several albums and star in the Broadway production of *The Color Purple*. In her memoir *Life Is Not a Fairy Tale*, she discusses her rape. When she was fourteen, Fantasia was assaulted by a boy at school. The aftermath of this event led to her dropping out of school and moving out of her family's home. She became a single mom at the age of seventeen. Fantasia was nineteen when she won *America Idol*.[f]

Teri Hatcher: She starred in the TV show *Desperate Housewives* and had vocal roles in the animated movies *Coraline* and *Planes*. In 2006 she spoke for the first time about being molested by her uncle at the age of seven. Teri Hatcher has since stated that she originally blamed herself for the sexual abuse and did not tell anyone for several years. She is now an activist and spoke at the United Nation's Official Commemoration of the

International Day for the Elimination of Violence against Women in New York City in 2014.[9]

Ashley Judd: Actress Ashley Judd has been starring in films and TV shows for two decades, most recently she played Natalie Prior in *Divergent*. She has also become increasingly public about her history of sexual abuse and has become an activist. Ashley says her healing journey began in 2006. Her memoir, *All That Is Bitter and Sweet*, shares details of her abuse.[h]

Lady Gaga: In 2013, Lady Gaga revealed that her song "Swine" was about rape, but didn't elaborate much beyond saying that she was raped when she was nineteen by a man twenty years older than her. In 2015 she sang the song "Til It Happens to You" with Diane Warren. The song was used in the documentary *The Hunting Ground*, which is about sexual assault on college campuses.[i] The song was nominated for an Oscar, and Lady Gaga gave a powerful performance of the song at the 2016 Oscars. She has since spoken about some of the effects that her rape has had on her.[j]

Oprah: Oprah was raped at the age of nine by a nineteen-year-old cousin who was supposed to be babysitting her and her two younger half siblings. She was then molested between the ages of ten and fourteen. At fourteen she became pregnant, but the baby boy died two weeks after birth. At sixteen, Oprah read Maya Angelou's book *I Know Why the Caged Bird Sings*, and has reported reading that book over and over again. She was able to overcome sexual abuse, has become one of the world's most successful women, and has interviewed many other survivors about their experiences.[k]

Tyler Perry: After his mother's death in 2009, Tyler Perry began to speak out publicly about the physical abuse he suffered at the hands of his father while he was growing up. Then in 2010 he spoke publicly on *The Oprah Winfrey Show* about being molested as a child. He expressed hope that by speaking out he would be giving other male survivors the courage to speak out as well.[l]

Gabrielle Union: In 2014, actress Gabrielle Union talked about her experience being raped at gun point at the age of nineteen. She was working in a Payless Shoes store when it was robbed, and during the robbery she was raped. In her experience, she emphasized the need she felt to stop being a victim and be a survivor.[m]

Queen Latifah: The singer-turned-actress is usually very private, but in 2013 she began to speak up about her history of childhood sexual abuse. When she was five, she was molested by a babysitter. Queen Latifah has said that because of her molestation, she has had relationship problems and trouble getting close to people. She has also been in therapy to recover from the trauma.[n]

Some victims of sexual assault spend a great deal of time thinking about to whom and how to disclose what happened. Others find themselves just blurting it out.[33] In either situation the victim is seeking help, a way to make sense of what has happened to him or her. The following story from Kelli shows how not disclosing the assault delayed her healing process and kept her from services needed to treat her for the depression and other psychological problems she experienced as a result of the trauma of being raped:

When I was thirteen and for as long as I can remember beforehand my one true love was basketball. Well, dancing and basketball. But mostly basketball. I was a diehard Michael Jordan fan and my favorite team was the Denver Nuggets (which is a story in itself). I was a straight A student, an avid reader, and I loved poetry and drawing. My mother was proud of me with one exception. She hated my love for basketball. My mom thought basketball was solely for boys. But when you're a girl growing up with only brothers, what choice did I have but to love the game? Every minute I spent outside the classroom was spent on the court. My dream was to be the first female in the NBA (way before the WNBA).

At school I had an awesome basketball coach. At first, I couldn't stand him. He was always pushing me harder and making me do routines over and over again until I perfected it. Once I started to see that I was getting better, I started to like and admire him. I worked harder to hear his praise and constantly sought out his recognition. That year our team won the finals. I'm not vain enough to say that we won because of my skill but because he built up a great team. We played well together. That year in eighth grade was one of the best school years of my life. I was sorry to see it end.

At the end of the school year, we all got yearbooks. The basketball team had a yearbook signing session complete with pizza and music. I forgot and left my book at home. I voiced my disappointment that my book wouldn't be signed by many of my teammates but most of all, my coach. He recommended that I come back one day that week so he could sign it.

One day after school, I went to the gym and asked him to sign my yearbook. We were alone as the basketball season was over and no one was expected to be there. He threw the ball into the overhang and I ran up to get it. He followed me. Up there, he pushed me on the mats. I can't even let my mind go back over that moment without anxiety and fear. He raped me.

Immediately afterwards, I walked home and threw up along the way. I got home and cleaned myself up. No one was home. I vowed never to tell anyone. I burned the clothes I was wearing and threw away my basketball and promised that I would never play again.

The experience deeply impacted my life. However, I think the secret was even more destructive than the rape itself. I stopped talking. In eighth grade, I was an honors student and class salutatorian. I participated in all types of extra-curricular activities from dancing in talent shows to playing basketball. I participated in spelling bees and math competitions (both school and statewide) and volunteered for the local Meals on Wheels program. I was actively involved in church and in the local community. After the experience, in ninth grade, I was barely a C student. I did everything I could to blend in and not stand out as much as possible. I was afraid that if I stood out in any way, I would attract attention and I would find myself getting hurt again. I lost my faith in God. I hated God for allowing me to dwell in the pain that I was in. I was angry that He didn't protect me. I felt abandoned and rejected so in turn I abandoned and rejected my own faith.

In tenth grade, I "forgot" what happened to me. My grades improved: I became an A student again. I volunteered in the community. However, I kept my promise and did not play basketball though I did become a cheerleader. I made plans to go to college. But my secret would always manifest at night. I had terrible nightmares where I relived my rape over and over again. I refused to sleep at night and avoided rest as much as possible. I couldn't stand to be touched especially on my bare skin. I lived this way for almost twenty years. I became more and more depressed. I pushed away family and friends and in hindsight, I see that I was punishing myself for my experience. I felt ashamed and guilty. I was tired. I was sad. Eventually I didn't want to live anymore. I couldn't handle the secret any longer. Though I was refusing to accept it and face it, it was still wearing me down.

One day I made the decision to end my life. I began to put my affairs in order. I wrote my will and began to give away some of my more personal belongings. I knew I had to put myself right with God before I ended my life. I went to church for the first time in almost twenty years. Once I got there, one of the ministers (my own personal miracle) approached me to welcome me and sensed my anguish. We talked for hours before I was finally able to voice what had been plaguing me for years: I was raped. From there, he recommended I go to therapy and he and I check in now and then.

My healing process has been slow. I imagined that once I started therapy I would be okay in just a few months. Yet three months later I'm still in therapy. I was diagnosed with PTSD. I'm much happier than I was three years ago. I smile and talk more. Instead of endings, my world is now full of possibilities. I'm in my first long-term loving relationship. I still have struggles. Even the most loving touches can trigger my fight-or-flight response. I try my best not to be seen. I write poetry and each time I speak at an open mic, I have to pray my way through it. Part of me is still afraid that if I'm seen, I will be harmed. I have a great support team to help me through these moments of fear, including my pastor, friends, my boyfriend, and even coworkers. When I'm ready to meet a milestone, they push me and support me until I reach my goals. However, I have never picked up a basketball again and I'm scared to do so.

Why did I write this? I wrote all of this for the sake of survivors. If I could change the past, I would say that I wish I was never raped obviously. But I can't change that. One thing I can change is the secret. Please don't keep your assault a secret. When people tell you that what happened was not your fault, believe them. No matter what you said or did, you don't deserve it. Don't allow that one moment in time to permanently define you. Today, by writing this I took the first step from being Kelli the Victim to Kelli the Survivor. Despite how hard it is, talk to someone about how you're feeling. [34]

VICTIM BLAMING AND OTHER RAPE MYTHS

Myths are generated through culture and religion, and are generally seen as humans' attempt to make sense of the world. Rape myths serve to separate women and men from the realities of sexual assault. In rape myths, men do not get raped. In rape myths, only certain women get raped. A woman can avoid getting raped if she dresses a certain way, if she doesn't drink, if she doesn't go to the wrong places. Rape myths also serve to justify sexual aggression from men. Rapists are different from regular men. It's not rape if she's drinking or if she's a tease. Men cannot stop or control themselves when they start to get sexually aroused, so if a woman turns on a man, she should expect to be raped. Women ask to be raped by making these choices. And even if a woman says no initially, she really enjoys being raped.[1] Such rationalization allows a rapist to consider himself guiltless of committing a serious crime, and women are able to feel distant from and superior to rape victims. These myths are supported by American culture and can be found in advertising, commercials, TV shows, movies, music, and books.

Rape Script

A lot of people believe in a rape script. A rape script is a very specific definition of rape. Rape scripts are also often referred to as "real rape," implying that assaults that don't fit this narrow definition aren't real. In a rape script, the rape occurs in a deserted public place. The perpetrator uses violence, perhaps even a weapon, and the victim is modestly dressed, completely sober, and usually virginal.[2] The rapist is deranged, or a druggie, or there is something wrong with him socially to the point that rape is the only way he can get a woman.[3] It's not a realistic portrayal of sexual assault, but it's what comes to mind for most people when they hear the word *rape*.

This type of rape, in which the woman is attacked outdoors by a stranger with a weapon, is commonly known as a blitz rape and is just one type of rape or sexual

Some Girls Are
by Courtney Summers

Regina is one of five popular girls who run the high school . . .

> Until she's not.
>
> Until her friend Anna thinks Regina seduced Anna's boyfriend at a party.
>
> But that's not what happened. The truth is that she was nearly raped, but no one believes her, and she has gone from being a bully to being the one who is bullied. The novel *Some Girls Are* is a vivid example of both slut shaming and victim blaming.[a]

---

assault, as has been previously described in this book. In the majority of sexual assaults, however, the victim knows the assailant.

Rape scripts are modeled by the media, in both TV sitcoms and movies. Media portray men's masculinity as being measurable by their sexual conquests.[4] TV dramas like *NCIS* and *Law & Order: Special Victims Unit* focus on and portray rapes that closely resemble preconceived notions of what a "real" rape looks like. Acquaintance rape, date rape, and sexual assault in relationships are not validated by the media as legitimate rape. This reflects societal attitudes, but it also amplifies those attitudes by reinforcing them and confirming for viewers that this is what "real" rape looks like.

The influence of rape scripts is seen in the criminal prosecution of sexual offenders. Sexual assaults that more closely resemble a classic rape script are more likely to lead to a conviction and to jail time than rapes that involve alcohol or drugs or sexual assaults that are perpetrated by someone the victim knows.[5] Conviction and jail time are also more likely if the perpetrator is black and the victim is white, because this also conforms to preconceived rape scripts that rapists are usually black and that "real" victims are white.[6]

Rape scripts also affect the victims and how they perceive what has happened to them. A woman who strongly believes in a blitz rape script and who experiences a sexual assault that doesn't fit in with that rape script may not even recognize that she has been raped. She will still experience the psychological harm of having been raped, but because she doesn't identify the event as a rape she won't report it, and she most likely won't seek the help she needs to begin her recovery.[7]

Victim Blaming

For some individuals, it's hard to understand what has happened when a sexual assault has occurred. Some people ask assault victims questions like "What were you wearing?" "Were you drinking?" "Why were you out so late?" There is a tendency to question whether an assault has occurred and to put part or all of the blame for the assault onto the victim. At the same time there is a lessening of the blame attributed to the perpetrator.[8]

While sexual assault does happen to both men and women, boys and girls, women are victimized at a higher rate, with about one in six American women being assaulted, compared to one in thirty-three American men.[9] And research shows that men are more likely than women to blame women for being victims of sexual assault. Psychologists believe that one reason for blaming victims is *just world belief*, or the belief that bad things only happen to people who deserve it. A just world belief is a deeply held worldview that life is just and fair. If you are a good person, good things happen to you. If you're a bad person, then bad things will happen to you. People who hold a just world belief have a hard time understanding when things happen for no apparent reason or when tragedy strikes too close to home. To maintain a just world view, the person has to find a way to rationalize the event, and this in some cases leads to victim blaming. The victim must have done something wrong, or such a horrible thing would not have happened to her.[10]

People will also take into consideration whether the person fought back or simply said no. It is a natural reaction for an individual to freeze during a sexual assault, but some interpret this freezing as not resisting and then blame the victim for being assaulted.[11]

Take, for instance, the popular question "What were you wearing?" Women dress the way they do for a variety of reasons, usually out of a desire to appear and feel attractive. However, sometimes a desire to look attractive is misrepresented as a desire to seduce or initiate sex.[12] Perpetrators of sexual assault will sometimes try to use a victim's attire as a defense for their actions. But no outfit, no matter how provocative, is ever a justification for sexual assault. Clothing is not consent to have sex.[13]

Alcohol and drugs are involved in a lot of sexual assaults. Many perpetrators of sexual assault will push alcoholic beverages onto a potential victim with the intent to get the victim intoxicated.[14] Consent for sexual acts cannot be given by someone who is intoxicated. However, when a person who is intoxicated is sexually assaulted there's a tendency to blame the victim for the assault.[15] This is another example of victim blaming.

About 68 percent of sexual assaults go unreported.[16] One reason for this is that victims sometimes blame themselves for the sexual assault. They are in fact victim blaming. Because they question whether their own actions may have brought on the rape or sexual assault, they are less likely to report the crime or to seek help.[17]

Victim blaming happens on an institutional level as well as on individual levels. Certain subcultures and environments blame victims, or may seek to silence them.

In December of 2014 the independent Christian organization GRACE (Godly Response to Abuse in the Christian Environment) released a report that was the end result of a two-year investigation of the fundamentalist Christian college Bob Jones University (BJU), which is located in Greenville, South Carolina. BJU requested the investigation after several allegations of sexual assault cases being mishandled drew public attention.

The college employs a biblical counseling model, which is supported by several tenured faculty members. Biblical counseling, as taught at BJU, treats a person's emotional distress as a symptom of the individual not being right with God because of sin. While this approach may help in some cases, it is not an effective treatment for trauma. None of the counselors have adequate training, and the report revealed that a large percentage of sexual assault victims who sought counseling on campus were questioned extensively about their sexual history, what they were wearing at the time of the assault, if they had been drinking or using drugs, and if they enjoyed the sexual assault. Some trauma symptoms, such as nightmares, were attributed to sinful thoughts or a choice on the part of the victim. Victims were also pressured to quickly forgive the perpetrator and to avoid the sin of "bitterness." The report included several accounts from victims about counselors pressuring them to identify actions that made them partially accountable for the sexual assault and encouraging them to repent of any sins that caused the assault. In an environment that places a high value on virginity, especially the virginity of women, sexual assault victims were often seen and represented as being "damaged goods" and as no longer being marriage material.[18]

The report concluded with detailed recommendations that BJU should take to make the campus a safer place for survivors of sexual assault and to provide better services to survivors. One of the most important recommendations was for the school to refer all victims of sexual assault to an off-campus trained trauma counseling service.[19]

Many of the Bob Jones students and former students who participated in the study were optimistic that this independent report would lead to real changes for the university atmosphere. Then in March 2015 university president Steve Pettit gave a speech addressing the university's plans for handling sexual assault going forward. While this speech outlines several positive changes that are being made by the university, including additional training for students and faculty members on sexual assault and abuse, the president also emphasized a strong commitment to continue the usage of biblical counseling for all student problems, including students who have been sexually assaulted.[20]

In the following story, Tiffany shares her experience with victim blaming. Notice how it took place in conjunction with other rape myths:

For most of my young adult life, I was a professional entertainer. I would travel, compete, and perform as a figure skater and ballroom dancer. At the age of eighteen, I moved in with a well-known coach and her husband. My goal was to represent the United States and Philippines in the next Olympics as a figure skater. Being raised in a conservative household, my parents have always told me to respect those that are older than you. I took this belief system with me when I moved in with my coach and her husband. Although I was eighteen years old, I was very naive and innocent. During this time, I was training in the mornings and working on my college degree during the day. My coach's husband worked from home so I would see him after training. He asked me what my interests are and if I had a boyfriend. He slowly started to gain my trust. Since my dad was busy at work, I started looking at my coach's husband like a father figure. I wanted to learn from him, especially since he had his own business.

Once he gained my trust, he started to take advantage of me sexually and mentally. This turned my world completely upside down. I became depressed, lost weight, and had no sense of reality. My skating started to suffer and eventually I decided to go home. Once I got home, I told my parents and at first, they didn't believe me. They thought that if something really happened, I should have said something from the very beginning. They even blamed me for what had happened. This took a big toll on me and I started seeing a therapist. My friends and family didn't understand what had happened and I felt completely alone. Thankfully, I had a therapist that understood my situation and she helped me move past this adversity.[21]

Women Lie

Acceptance of the rape myths already discussed, that real rape follows the script of a blitz rape and that some women ask to be raped by their behavior, leads to the confirmation of another rape myth: women lie about rape.

In this myth, a woman engages in consensual sex and then later regrets it or wants to "punish" the man and ruin his life by claiming that she was raped. In reality, research shows that only about 2 to 8 percent of rape reports are false, similar to false reports for other crimes. Acceptance of this myth is very broad, and it can affect both how police interview and treat victims and how the legal system handles a rape case. If the rape doesn't involve a weapon, if there are no serious

Victim Blaming in Advertising

The following is an essay by Ashley, a college freshman.

Preventing a Danger or Promoting a Crime?

Feminists all over the country coined the term "rape culture" nearly forty-five years ago. But it wasn't until I came across an advertisement published by the Pennsylvania Liquor Control Board (PLCB) several years ago, that I became familiar with the term too. This advertisement sparked so much controversy that, shortly after its publication, it resulted in its removal from circulation. This image presents a young woman laying on what looks like a bathroom floor, with her underwear around her ankles, and it reads "She didn't want to do it, but she couldn't say no." This presents a prime example of how rape culture is promoted in today's society through two behaviors that are commonly associated with it: victim-blaming and normalizing sexual abuse.

Victim-blaming takes place when an innocent person is believed to be responsible for a crime that was committed against them. This idea is rooted from the belief that actions have predictable consequences, therefore people are responsible for and in control of what happens to them. The PLCB writes "When your friends drink, they can end up making bad decisions, like going home with someone they don't know very well. Decisions like that leave them vulnerable to dangers like date rape . . ." So the decisions of a woman determine whether her being sexually assaulted is justified or not. Because if those decisions left her vulnerable to rape, then the crime committed against her is no longer considered a crime, but a mere consequence? Is this outrageous or what?

This advertisement completely ignores who is really to blame for a crime like rape. Instead of teaching how to prevent being raped, why don't we teach not to rape? Maybe we could try teaching men not to take advantage of a woman's vulnerability. "She didn't want to do it, but she couldn't say no" so because she didn't actually say no, the perpetrator is in his own right to sexually abuse her? This is telling me that when a woman is inebriated and vulnerable, she will no longer be able to avoid being raped. Ignore the fact that her speech was impaired or that she may have blacked out due to her alcohol intoxication, it's her responsibility to avoid being raped by saying "no." This image is telling people all around the world that rape happens because women allow it to. I don't think that victim-blaming can get any clearer than this.

Normalization has frequently been a strategy used to encourage rape culture. This idea is rooted from the belief that rape is a normal consequence for a woman's actions. Normalizing sexual abuse goes hand-in-hand with victim-blaming. In fact, victim-blaming wouldn't be so common if sexual abuse wasn't perceived as something normal in today's society. In this advertisement, the PLCB calls date rape a mere "danger," as though it is something that can so easily be prevented. Rape is not a danger. Riding in the car without your seat belt on is a danger. Rape is a crime. It's simple. There is a perpetrator and there is a victim. This advertisement was not made to prevent a danger such as a car accident. This was made to promote a crime. To encourage people into believing that it's a normal consequence when you don't take precaution.

In this ad, the PLCB refuses to acknowledge that a decision such as drinking is not an invitation for sexual abuse. Instead, they put all of their effort into not just blaming the victim (and oddly even the victim's friends) for the result of their decisions but also into portraying rape as an everyday consequence. Because of images such as these that promote rape culture, women in all parts of the world choose to not just remain quiet about being sexually assaulted, but also become manipulated into believing that they are to blame. Images such as these desensitize people. They enhance people's predisposition towards rape, creating a tendency to view rape as a minor offense that can easily be prevented. It is completely illogical to view rape how rape culture intends for us to view it. We don't blame a victim of theft for deciding to go to the mall with cash in their wallet. We don't blame the many children who are victims of kidnapping every day for walking home from the bus stop. So why blame victims of rape because of their vulnerability? None of these examples are just a normal danger, none of the victims are to blame, and none of their actions invite or justify the crime.

I first came across this advertisement back in 2011, but it wasn't until several days prior to writing this that I decided to really sit down and interpret what it means to me. I came across a multitude of other interpretations, all ranging from "the truth is that rape is a fact of life and women must protect themselves from it" to my personal favorite, which takes the original advertisement and re-words it to read "Rape is wrong and so is victim-blaming. When your friends use alcohol as a weapon, they can end up targeting and sexually violating people unable to consent. Decisions like that make them rapists." My personal belief is that the most effective way to prevent crimes like rape, is to start prosecuting the ones who are really responsible for it. To point our finger at the perpetrator and not the victim, and hold them accountable for the severity of their crime. Unfortunately, advertisements such as these that encourage and promote victim-blaming and normalization of sexual abuse continue floating around the Internet. Until these images and ideas are removed from society, rape culture will continue to prevail.[b]

injuries, and if the perpetrator is someone the victim knows, then the case does not fit the blitz rape script that many people believe in. For the jury, seeing a case that does not fit a classic rape script can lead them to conclude that the woman is lying; the acceptance of one rape myth leads to the acceptance of another.[22]

This is another rape myth that is supported by the media. For example, when DNA evidence proves that someone was falsely accused and convicted of rape, it makes national news. It makes national news because it is a rare occurrence. Because it is a well-reported event, it gives people the wrong impression that such false accusation and imprisonment is common rather than a surprising event. For individuals who already believe that women lie about rape, this confirms their belief systems and helps them become even more greatly entrenched in rape myth acceptance.[23]

In Alaska, defendants who are accused of sexual assault or child sexual abuse can call the victim's creditability into question by bringing up any other times

Acceptance of rape culture can lead a victim of sexual assault to feel that the assault was her fault.

the victim may have filed sexual assault charges that did not lead to a prosecution. Such a legal policy seems designed to sabotage the justice system, given that rape is falsely reported at roughly the same rate as other crimes, that those who have been sexually assaulted are at a greater risk of being re-victimized, and that prosecution rates for sexual assault are extremely low. It also speaks of a broad legal acceptance of the rape myth that women lie about being raped and that they will lie about it multiple times.[24]

Minimization/Denial

There is a tendency to play down the severity of sexual assault, and to downplay its potential to cause the victim lasting harm. Acceptance of other rape myths, including a rape script and victim blaming, leads to a great tendency to downplay the seriousness of sexual assault. Also, the better acquainted the perpetrator is with the victim, the less serious the assault will be considered. If the perpetrator and the victim once dated, for instance, and if they were drinking, even if the victim says no and resists, some people will deny that a sexual assault even took place.[25]

The victim may also minimize or deny that a sexual assault has occurred, especially in the context of a relationship. The realization of what has happened

Rape Girl by Alina Klein

Valerie is now known as one thing—the girl who said she was raped. No one seems to believe her. This novel follows the reporting and the legal process, and illustrates the disbelief that victims face when they report a rape. *Rape Girl* is also about a survivor who learns to overcome extreme trials. This is Alina Klein's first novel.[c]

may only come later. A victim's acceptance of rape myths contributes to minimization and denial.[26]

Sex offenders also have a tendency to deny or minimize that they have committed a crime and that their actions have caused someone harm. Sometimes this type of denial or minimization can prevent the offender from receiving care and treatment. Studies have shown that minimization and denial in sex offenders is often rooted in rape myth acceptance.[27]

The tendency to deny or to minimize the seriousness of sexual assault is not limited to the victims and perpetrators. As national attention has been raised about how widespread the problem of sexual assault is, there has also been an effort from some groups and individuals to downplay and deny the statistics on sexual assault and the scope of the problem.

For example, in 2011 *USA Today* ran an article entitled "College Women Don't Get Wasted on Campus" in which the author argued that the statistics that one in five college women have been raped are exaggerated, and that researchers are simply deciding at random who has and has not been raped. The author, Naomi Schaefer Riley, does not take into account that victims may blame themselves for the assault and not identify the trauma symptoms they experience as being a result of a rape. Indeed, Riley seems to imply that researchers wish to bloat the numbers of rape victims for some unknown purpose, rather than simply identifying victims who fit a set of predetermined criteria that meet the definition of rape. At the same time, she cites research on the number of reported college rapes that involved alcohol, implying that rape is caused by drinking.[28] This ignores the fact that behind every rape, there is a rapist. If victim A decides to go home early from the bar to "stay safe," a rapist is most likely going to move on to victim B. While there is some merit to encouraging women to be careful when out drinking in public, that does nothing to actually address the problem. And until the rape culture and other rape myths stop, this culture will continue to prevent victims from identifying the source of the trauma they have experienced as rape, and there will be a continued need for researchers to use unbiased criteria to identify instances of sexual assault.

Rape Myths about People of Color

The oversexualizing of women of color, especially black women, has a long history. Native women have been sexually exploited by Europeans since the latter arrived, and black slaves were also sexually exploited.[29] Women of color are seen as hypersexual and available. Black women are seen as sexually available and promiscuous. Asian women are seen as sexual and submissive. Latina women are also seen as being sexually available. Native women are victimized at a much higher rate than women from other races, and nine times out of ten the assailant is not Native.[30] Additionally, domestic violence, including sexual assault, has become a widespread problem in all Native communities. The creation of this current problem has been attributed to colonization and the introduction to Western power structures. Some advocate groups are pushing for a culturally sensitive solution, one that would include a return to traditional Native values and the re-institution of the sacredness of women.[31]

Rape myths about women of color may prevent them from seeking help. The stigma and the fear of not being believed can prevent them from reporting. Additionally, a sense of community could also lead these victims to not report; for example, a black woman, knowing how black men are already seen as criminals, may be hesitant to report a sexual assault from a black man.[32]

Because women of color are marginalized and are less likely to be believed when reporting a sexual assault, they are particularly vulnerable to become victims.

In November 2015, Daniel Holtzclaw went on trial for sexually assaulting thirteen women while on duty as a police officer in a poorer, predominately black neighborhood in Oklahoma City. His victims ranged in age from seventeen to fifty-seven, and all of them were black. Holtzclaw was dismissed from the Oklahoma City Police Department in January 2015 after multiple complaints. It appears clear that Holtzclaw targeted his victims because they were black and poor, and some of them had records for drugs or prostitution. He knew that these women were not likely to report the assault, and if they did report it, they were not likely to be believed. Holtzclaw was right; the case was only prosecuted after many complaints. During the trial, the defense, when cross-examining the victims, made it a point to emphasize any legal issues in their past.[33] Holtzclaw was convicted of eighteen counts of sexual abuse, among them four counts of first degree rape. He was sentenced to serve 263 years in prison.[34]

With this case, it became easier to prosecute because of the number of women who came forward. Even though these women were part of a marginalized group, their sheer numbers added to their credibility. When police officers and prosecutors decide which cases to pursue, one of the things they consider is the likelihood of the case leading to a conviction. If the victim does not seem credible or does not seem to fit into the stereotyped rape-script victim image, police and prosecutors may be less committed to investigating and pursuing a legal case and may even discourage the victim from pressing charges or pursuing justice through the legal system.[35]

Silencing

The previous chapter discussed some of the challenges to speaking up about sexual assault. However, many of the rape myths discussed in this chapter also prevent victims from speaking up. Certain communities, including some religious communities, put pressure on their members to be silent about sexual abuse. Additionally, rape myths specific to people of color also serve to silence them.

In religious communities that are insular in nature, victims are silenced in several ways. When the perpetrator is in a position of ecclesiastic authority, there is a tendency for members of the community to not believe the victim, thereby shutting the victim down. There is also a desire by both community members and religious authorities to handle things internally and to protect the overall image of the community. There could also be some distrust of secular authorities.

All of these factors came into play in 2012 when an eighteen-year-old girl from the Orthodox Jewish Satmar Hasidic community of Brooklyn testified in the trial of the man who had sexually abused her for three years, from the age of twelve to fifteen. The perpetrator, Nechemya Weberman, was an unlicensed therapist who had regular meetings with the girl in order to give her lessons on being more religious. He was convicted of fifty-nine counts of sexual abuse, including acting out a pornographic video, oral sex, and groping. The community response has been very hard on the victim and her family. Overall there is a deep disbelief that the abuse actually took place, possibly because of Weberman's standing in the community. There is also anger that this case was reported and prosecuted by secular authorities rather than being handled within the community. The fact that this case led to a conviction and jail time has added to the distrust the Orthodox Jewish Satmah Hasidic community already had for the police and the legal system.[36]

Rape Culture in Music

Rape culture is found in all forms of media, including in music. Here are just a few examples:

Avril Lavigne, "Smile": This song is mostly a love song, but it also describes date rape. The singer sings about blacking out and asks her love interest what he put in her drink. She is not upset by possibly being drugged by the guy she likes; instead, the incident is portrayed as a positive thing in this up-beat song, which is another danger of rape culture. Will portrayals like this convince women that being drugged by a man is a good thing?[d]

Maroon 5, "Animals": Shortly after its release, fans expressed outrage at the music video, which depicts blood, lots of stalking—taking photographs while stalking, breaking and entering by the stalker—and then sex. Basically the video is a stalker's fantasy. The Rape, Abuse and Incest National Network even criticized the video. Maroon 5 released a new video, this one featuring snakes and a bunny, but that does nothing to correct the problematic lyrics of the song, which match the original video and tell the story of stalking, portraying it as romantic and implying that it's something the woman wants.[e]

Robin Thicke, "Blurred Lines": The lyrics in this song present the idea that consent is a "blurry" concept. It's implied, although not stated, that the girl he's singing to has said no, but the phrase "you know you want it" is repeated throughout the song. At the end, some marijuana is brought up, and the singer mentions how it's "always worked" for him, which seems to imply using it to get the girl high in order to rape her.[f]

Carrie Underwood, "Before He Cheats": While the song is mostly about a woman seeking revenge after her boyfriend cheated on her, the singer describes the scenario that may be going on inside the bar. When her boyfriend's date says that she's drunk, the guy's reaction is to think he's going to "get lucky," or have sex. This song feeds into the date rape myth that it's acceptable to have sex with someone who is intoxicated, even if she is unable to give consent. This song, while reflecting cultural norms, is reinforcing rape culture by showing potential date rape as a normal event.[g]

Are songs about sexual assault, and songs that support rape culture, a new phenomenon? Are these types of songs a passing trend? Not at all. One such song, originally written in 1944, has stood the test of time, and is played repeatedly every December. The song "Baby, It's Cold Outside" is written as a duet, and instead of designating roles as male or female, in the original sheet music the parts were attributed as "mouse" and "wolf," which in itself says a lot about the roles of these two people. Traditionally the woman is the mouse and keeps saying how she needs to go home. The man, or wolf, keeps trying to persuade her to stay. The prolonged pressure in itself implies coercion, but then the woman asks what the man put in her drink, which implies date rape. The message of this song seems to be that it's okay to disregard what your romantic interest is saying; just keep pressuring him or her to stay. Oh, and it's okay to spike a drink, too. It has been argued that in the time the song was written, it was actually very progressive for a woman to consider staying the night, but even so, her partner's disregard for what she's saying is troubling. Also, even though this is a song from another era, given the objectionable lyrics, why are we still playing it on the radio with Christmas music? It actually isn't a Christmas song, but it gets played with the general holiday mix. The continued popularity of "Baby, It's Cold Outside" seems to reflect the popularity and acceptance of coercion tactics and the usage of date rape drugs.[h]

Rape Culture

All of the rape myths make up our rape culture. A rape culture is when violence against women is treated as normal and is even supported; sexual violence is viewed as being inevitable. Rape culture is made up of music, media, and jokes that normalize or trivialize sexual assault. The acceptance of sexual violence is also reflected in the legal system, in how sexual assault cases are handled, and in the sentences actually served by criminals. As noted previously, very few offenders will ever spend a day in jail. There have been several cases when news reports have sympathized with young men convicted of rape, lamenting that this one "mistake" ruined this young man's life. News reports like these ignore the fact that this one "mistake" was actually a choice, and that choice ruined someone else's life as well, someone whose choice was taken.[37] That is rape culture. It is seen in romantic movies, when the boy just won't leave the girl alone, even when she asks him to. It is a manifestation of the belief that women fantasize about rape, that when women say no they really mean yes, and that women enjoy being sexually assaulted—that it is romantic.[38] That's rape culture. It's also in how we depict sexual acts in pornography. In pornography sexual violence and sexual coercion are portrayed as normal, and violence against women, especially sexual violence, is shown as being "hot."[39] That's rape culture.

Facebook

One place that daily plays out the acceptance of rape culture is social media. On Facebook, for example, it's permissible to post a meme that contains a rape joke. It's also acceptable to post images of violence against women, like the image of a man pushing a woman down some stairs because of an unwanted pregnancy. Facebook allows pages devoted to "teen slut pictures." But Facebook draws the line at images of a woman breastfeeding, or pictures of post-mastectomy scars, or even a cupcake with icing designed to look like labia. Those images are too offensive. When questioned about these types of decisions, Facebook representatives simply said that while they try to limit the amount of offensive material, anything that is not offensive and harmful is allowed, because they don't want to limit free speech.[40]

Facebook is not unique; it's a reflection of popular societal attitudes. So think on that a moment: A woman nursing her baby is harmful. The scars of a cancer

Rape culture and societal pressure can lead young men to have low self-esteem.

survivor are harmful. A cupcake is harmful. But memes of rape jokes and women being abused—those are just good fun and games. That is rape culture.

Rape culture isn't just harmful to women; it's harmful and insulting to men as well. Rape culture says that men only want one thing and will do anything to get it. Rape culture says that men have no self-control, and once they are aroused, they cannot stop themselves. Rape culture supports an image of masculinity that is animalistic and says that men who don't conform to that image are weak.[41]

Countering the Rape Culture

As more people become aware of the dangers of rape culture attitudes, people are beginning to take action to combat them.

On the last page of *Ms. Magazine*, for example, are ads that degrade or insult women. This page is called "No Comment." It simply contains a picture of the advertisement, the name of the ad, and the contact information for the company that distributed the ad. The purpose of this page is to get readers to write to that company to complain about the offensive advertisement. Many ads that support or promote rape culture have been taken down as a result of this ongoing campaign, and one would hope that the companies that have run such ads are subsequently more careful in how they promote their merchandise.[42]

Some forms of protest to rape culture are more dramatic. On January 24, 2011, Toronto police constable Michael Sanguinetti told a group of college students that women should avoid being raped by not dressing like sluts. His remarks led to outrage and then to activism. On April 2, 2011, a crowd of over three thousand marched through the streets of Toronto to the police station. Some of the protestors were dressed in regular clothes, while other chose to dress as "sluts." The protest of the police constable's words was the first SlutWalk, and since that time SlutWalks have been organized in many cities around the world.[43]

There are many other ways to take action against rape culture and sexual assault. The final chapter of this book will address these in greater detail.

SUPPORT FOR SURVIVORS

Survivors of sexual assault need the support of friends and family to aid them in their recovery. Research shows that receiving such support helps survivors avoid many of the health risks that are common for victims of sexual assault. Support also aids in faster emotional healing.[1] It can also help survivors avoid more severe psychological problems like post-traumatic stress disorder.[2] Survivors who experience positive reactions when they disclose their assault to others are less likely to engage in harmful coping behaviors like substance abuse.[3] Positive reactions and social support also can reduce levels of self-blaming and help a survivor's self-esteem.[4]

Sometimes survivors of sexual assault find that their friends and family are not as supportive as they would like. Or survivors may find that they are still struggling in their recovery. For these individuals it's important to reach out to other sources of support, such as organizations for assault survivors or local rape crisis centers.

In the following story, Deborah describes her struggle to find support from friends and family after being raped:

I was staying with my mom in her apartment over summer break during college, in my hometown of Massachusetts. It was July 4th. I went to the Boston Pops concert in Boston with some friends and got home late. My mom and her boyfriend at the time (she was divorced) were not home. I went to sleep. I woke up to someone on top of me raping me while another held me down. Then I was raped by a second one. They took turns holding my hands and head. I felt like I wasn't there as if I was watching over my body. Odd? I don't know. I know they were black and one had a hat. When they left I called my friend Caroline whose boyfriend was a cop or related to a cop, I don't remember. She later told me I was incredibly hysterical on the phone. No doubt. I remember talking to the police in the hospital afterwards. I gave them descriptions of the guys. I saw my mom

Sexual Assault Awareness Month (SAAM) History

In the late 1970s, a movement started in England. Women, fed up with street harassment and sexual assault, organized a protest: a march called Take Back the Night. The event raised awareness, and soon the idea spread to other countries. In 1978, the first Take Back the Night events were held in San Francisco and New York.

As support and awareness grew, in the late 1980s the National Coalition against Sexual Assault planned a week in April to promote educational campaigns on sexual assault. The campaign continued to grow, and by the late 1990s many events occurred throughout the month of April. In 2001, April officially became Sexual Assault Awareness Month (SAAM), complete with an official color (teal) and symbol (a teal ribbon). Each year a new campaign is developed. Past campaigns have focused on themes such as healthy relationships, sexual assault in the workplace, and sexual assault on campus. SAAM is the result of the efforts of several organizations and does a lot to educate and raise awareness. Along with general information and statistics, SAAM serves to inform people about what resources are available for survivors of sexual assault.[a]

on the way to the hospital and she was crying. I guess she found out from the police. She said "and you were a virgin." Or something like that. It was awkward. I said, "No mom, I was not a virgin. I had sex when I was a freshman." That was a strange conversation to have with your mom right after you were raped. I couldn't sleep for weeks, months afterward. I ran a lot. I'm not talking about jogging. I ran! With my music, at full blast. My mom, her boyfriend (now her husband), and my dad walked on eggshells around me. No one mentioned a thing. No one talked about it. If I brought it up, the subject was changed quickly. I never saw a therapist or psychiatrist or even talked with a friend. Sucky? Yup. For years the 4th of July brought hideous memories. Still does a little. . . .

I did suffer from PTSD and I wanted to talk to my mom but she refused. I would run or sleep. I didn't want to shop. We went out to a restaurant and I felt everyone was staring at me and knew about what happened.

I hated that thought. At night when I couldn't sleep I would drive my mother's car and go see Caroline at her job. She worked at a hospital (not the one I went too) and I would talk with her. I avoided sleep! My goal. I tended to sleep during the day, so I guess that was my way of coping.[5]

Finding the right support is especially difficult for sexual assault survivors who identify as LGBTQ (lesbian, gay, bisexual, transgender, queer/questioning). Staff at hospitals, rape crisis centers, and even police may not be trained or experienced in working with LGBTQ individuals. There is also a fear of encountering insensitivity or even outright hostility from the same people who are supposed to be providing help and support.[6] People of color who are victimized face similar challenges, including the risk of not being believed because of rape myth acceptance by care providers.[7] Some organizations either provide support specifically for people in these groups or have made it a point to have training to provide inclusive care for all victims of sexual assault.

Local support from rape crisis centers and other sexual assault organizations can provide many resources for sexual assault victims. These local organizations usually offer a range of services, including a volunteer to accompany a victim to the hospital, to the police station to file a report, even to court to provide emotional support. Many centers even have legal assistance for those wishing to report the assault. Local organizations also offer individual and group counseling, as well as support groups. Emergency shelter, education, and volunteer opportunities are also usually available. A searchable database of local centers can be found at the Rape, Abuse and Incest National Network (RAINN) at centers.rainn.org. RAINN also has a database in Spanish at centros.rainn.org.[8]

The following story is from a young woman who found support from both RAINN and from counseling. Toby, age nineteen, also talks about the support she has received from friends:

I have benefited tremendously from counseling and support groups. The biggest hurdle for me was definitely gaining the courage to ask for help. RAINN has a great online chat room that helps tremendously. I was able to find support groups that really help keep me balanced. Therapy isn't the most socially acceptable thing on the planet, but I've come to not be ashamed of it. If I got sick, I'd go to the doctor. If I broke my leg, no one would fault me for going to physical therapy a year later because I needed to rehabilitate my leg. But many people see counseling as a weakness, as if someone can just "conquer" their mental health setbacks. I am able to conquer my mental health problems, but only with the help of counseling. It makes me no less strong for taking on my demons. I'm still fighting them, this time, I'm just not doing it alone.

Support from other survivors can be very helpful.

Other sources to gain help from can be as simple as good friends. Some people won't support you during your recovery process, and that's totally fine. I've learned that the people who walked out when I needed them most opened the door for the people I truly value in my life. My friends provide me with such great support. They know some days are better than others, and I know the same about them. We have different struggles, but we're all united in the knowledge that we all struggle, yet all want the same thing in the end. We all want to give love, receive love, and be loved. Positive social networks like the ones I have are imperative.[9]

The following websites offer support to survivors. Use caution if you are currently being abused or stalked. Not all websites are secure.

- *1 in 6:* www.1in6.org. 1 in 6 offers support to men who have been sexually assaulted in childhood. This site provides information and support, including a live chat line that is available 24/7. The focus of this organization is to help male survivors heal and have healthier, happier lives.

The Mockingbirds
by Daisy Whitney

Set at a prestigious boarding school that claims perfection, *The Mockingbirds* tells the story of Alex, who is date raped while very drunk. The book portrays a toxic environment that is unwilling to acknowledge anything that might tarnish the school's reputation. Despite this setting, which is a realistic reflection of how some institutions handle sexual assault, Alex is able to find the support she needs from friends and from the secret vigilante society the Mockingbirds.

This is the debut novel from Daisy Whitney, who is a survivor of date rape.[b]

- *After Silence:* www.aftersilence.org. After Silence is an online support community. In addition to providing information on sexual assault, After Silence hosts thirty online message boards, a chat room, and functions as an online support group. Staff also respond to emails, and offer referrals to additional services. Most of the message boards are private, and require registration. After Silence provides support and help for all survivors of sexual assault, including men and those identifying as LGBTQ. For more about After Silence, see the "About Us" page (www.aftersilence.org/about-aftersilence.php).
- *Break the Cycle:* www.breakthecycle.org. Break the Cycle is committed to educating teens about dating violence and to helping them to break free from the cycle of abuse. This site provides information and resources for victims of teen dating violence, including victims of sexual assault.
- *INCITE! Women of Color against Violence:* www.incite-national.org. IN-CITE! is a national network that works to end violence against women. The organization describes itself as a group of "radical feminists of color": its focus is on grassroots organizing, creating dialogue, and promoting direct action to end sexual assault. INCITE! works to end violence, including sexual assault, against women, gender nonconforming, and trans people of color. The website has many articles and other resources promoting education and a critical social dialogue.
- *Joyful Heart Foundation:* www.joyfulheartfoundation.org. The Joyful Heart Foundation was founded by Mariska Hargitay, an actress on *Law and Order: Special Victims Unit* who was inspired by the storylines of the show to do something to help victims of sexual assault. Joyful Heart hosts

retreats and wellness days to help survivors of sexual assault on their path toward healing. The foundation also has an education campaign and publishes a magazine entitled *Reunion*. In conjunction with these educational efforts, there is an Engaging Men program. Joyful Heart Foundation also acts as an advocate, working to change laws and policies.

- *Male Survivor:* www.malesurvivor.org. Male Survivor offers support services for male survivors of sexual assault, including a chat room and discussion board. Both are secure and require registration. The organization also offers conferences and retreats to help with the healing process.
- *Minnesota Indian Women's Sexual Assault Coalition:* www.miwsac.org. While this organization is based in Minnesota, it provides contact information for resources for Native victims from several states. The site also offers links to informative articles, suggestions for self-care, and educational resources.
- *National Organization of Asians and Pacific Islanders Ending Sexual Violence:* www.napiesv.org. The website for this organization provides sexual assault information specific to Asian and Pacific Islander populations, both in the United States and in other countries. The site also has webinars on sexual assaults and ways to get involved to end sexual violence.
- *The National Organization of Sisters of Color Ending Sexual Assault (SCESA):* www.sisterslead.org. A national advocacy organization, SCESA provides support and training for organizations serving victims of color. The website has lists of both national and local organizations that support victims from different ethnic backgrounds, including Asian/Pacific Islander, Black/African American, Native American, and Latina.
- *National Sexual Violence Resource Center:* www.nsvrc.org. The National Sexual Violence Resource Center offers a wealth of research and information on sexual assault, including a searchable database of articles and recent studies.
- *Pandora's Project:* www.pandys.org. Pandora's Project offers a wide range of resources to survivors of sexual assault, including a message board, a chat room, a lending library, many online articles, and a resource list to help survivors find more help. The organization also sponsors weekend retreats for survivors. The goal of Pandora's Project is to make resources and support opportunities available to anyone who needs them, regardless of location or financial situation. Pandora's Project provides resources and support to teens and adults, men and women, and the LGBTQ community.
- *Rape, Abuse and Incest National Network (RAINN):* www.rainn.org. RAINN operates the National Sexual Assault Hotline at 1-800-656-HOPE and www.online.rainn.org. The online hotline also offers services in Spanish at www.rainn.org/es. RAINN has a searchable database that provides

information about local rape crisis centers and other sexual assault service providers. RAINN also works to educate about sexual assault and provides many chances for volunteerism, including the RAINN Speaker's Bureau, which gives survivors opportunities to share their story.

- *Safe Horizon:* www.safehorizon.org. Safe Horizon offers support for victims of family and community violence, including sexual assault. Safe Horizon also advocates for policies to prevent violence on the local, state, and national level. There is a twenty-four-hour hotline at 1-800-621-4673. You can also email at help@safehorizon.org; however, it may take up to seventy-two hours to receive a response.
- *Survivors Network of Those Abused by Priests (SNAP):* www.snapnetwork .org. SNAP is a national organization providing support groups for those who have been sexually abused by priests or other spiritual leaders. The site has a calendar of events that shows support group meetings in various areas throughout the United States. A secure login is required to access the calendar.
- *The Trevor Project:* www.thetrevorproject.org. This organization is focused on suicide prevention and support for LGBTQ teens and young adults. The Trevor Project offers many programs and raises awareness about LGBTQ youth. There is a crisis and suicide preventing hotline for LGBTQ teens and young adults (ages thirteen to twenty-four) available twenty-four hours a day at 1-866-488-7386.

The Invisible War

The documentary *The Invisible War* discusses sexual assault within the US military. A female officer in the armed forces is less likely to be shot by enemy fire than she is to be sexually assaulted by a fellow soldier. This documentary exposes the harsh reality faced by sexual assault victims in the military, including how rape and sexual assault cases are ignored or brushed aside, or how the victim is even punished for reporting the crime. Victims who are members of the armed forces are often isolated from support.

This documentary has received a lot of awards, including a 2014 Emmy Award for Best Documentary, a 2013 Emmy Award for Outstanding Investigative Journalism, and a 2013 George Foster Peabody Award.[c]

There are many online support groups available to help you in addition to your local rape crisis center.

This is by no means an exhaustive list of the resources that are available to survivors of sexual assault. Local crisis centers and counseling are also great places to start. With counseling it's important to find a counselor who has experience or training in working with people who have experienced sexual assault. It's also important to find the counselor who works best with your personality. If you have a bad experience with one counselor, it's a good idea to try working with another, until you find the right one.

The following is Destiny's experience with counseling:

After struggling in school and closing myself off from people for months, I was at a breaking point. I was so depressed, but knew I needed help. So I emailed one of my professors and asked her for advice. After speaking to that professor and an advisor from academic services, I was referred to the counseling center at my university. Counseling saved my life. I was able to talk about the abuse and other issues I was going through. I was diagnosed with Generalized Anxiety Disorder and my counselor went over strategies to overcome it. She re-assured me what happened wasn't my fault and I could be happy again. So she encouraged me to write down my dreams, focus on the present and surround myself with positive people and activities.

At first, I was hesitant to follow her instructions. During the first two months of counseling, I continued to seclude myself from others. I'd lie and tell her I was getting better, but she knew the truth. Getting through each day felt like wading through water with weights attached to my feet. It hurt like hell, but slowly I made it. It took a long time to believe in myself and venture out, but I did. After fifteen months of counseling, it was time to continue the healing process without my counselor. My counselor was moving away, so the counseling sessions came to an end. My counselor told me I'd come a long way and reminded me to use all of the tools, strategies, and advice she'd given me.[10]

HEALING AND RECOVERY

S exual assault causes trauma to the victim, and healing from such trauma takes time. Victims of childhood sexual assault are at a greater risk of developing post-traumatic stress disorder (PTSD) and of experiencing lifelong symptoms of PTSD.[1] It is also common for victims to feel a great sense of shame and self-blame.[2] Victims blame themselves as a way to try to understand the sexual assault and why it happened.[3] Survivors often suppress the emotions and thoughts from the assault through drug use, alcohol, keeping busy, and self-harm.[4] Healing from such trauma is possible.

For victims of childhood sexual assault, the trauma from the assault can alter their developing worldview. The assault impacts the child's belief system and how he views other people, whether basically good or bad; how he views fairness in life; and how he views himself. Survivors of childhood sexual assault often develop negative beliefs about themselves, such as viewing themselves as wrong or blaming themselves for the assault. It is easy for a child to take the shame and self-blame from a sexual assault and internalize those feelings. One of the reasons childhood sexual assault has such an impact is that it is often perpetrated by someone the child knows and trusts, and since the abuse occurs during important formative years it can cause lasting harm.[5]

Survivors of sexual assault may experience a disconnect from the experience. This is a way that the human mind can protect itself from trauma. The person may not fully remember the event, or it may seem like the assault happened to someone else. The victim will also not be able to recognize that negative thought patterns, such as self-blame and feelings of worthlessness, are caused by the sexual assault.[6] All of these psychological impacts are discussed more fully in chapter 5, "After the Assault."

In the following story, Claudia describes her experience with this kind of disconnect and how she was unable to address her abuse for years:

I grew up feeling that my father loved me. I don't know when that changed, when that became a sexual thing to him.

Self-Care after Sexual Assault

Taking care of yourself after a sexual assault is very important for your recovery. Just as there are physical and psychological impacts from a sexual assault, there are both physical and psychological ways to care for yourself to help with the healing process:

Physical self-care

- Eat healthy
- Exercise
- Get enough sleep
- Perform proper hygiene/grooming
- Avoid abusing substances

Psychological self-care

- Go to counseling or therapy
- Start journaling
- Engage in meditation

I forgot until I was nineteen. I woke up with my boyfriend one morning and it all came back to me. I didn't think anything of it, it was so long ago. That's when I started abusing drugs. Then when I was around twenty-seven I realized that none of my life was working. So I stopped using drugs and started going to therapy for the first time. Therapy made me capable of living, capable of getting a job. I finally earned enough money to start traveling, which I had always wanted to do. I could finally get a car loan, and buy a fancy car. I think after five years or so I stopped the therapy because I finally felt like I could take on life by myself.

For a long time before therapy, I was numb. I didn't want to feel anything. That's why I used the drugs. Whatever I felt was confusing and didn't help.

It took me years to see my feelings as being really valid.

You are important and you matter. Your voice matters, your feelings matter, your story matters, always.

If I had to say where I am on my healing journey, I'd say I'm not here nor there. I'm walking a path I hope to be proud of. I take the time to accept my faults and admit when I'm wrong. I also take the time to love myself and treat myself, whether that means allowing myself to eat a piece of chocolate or simply looking in the mirror and telling myself I'm beautiful. Self-care is extremely important, and shouldn't be neglected on a survivor's journey to healing. It's easy to dedicate ourselves to a project instead of taking care of ourselves. In the immediate aftermath of my assault, I volunteered about 40 hours a week while still attending high school full time. It's easy to throw yourself into something you believe is bigger than yourself. It's much harder to take a step back and realize that you're the one who needs help. It's easy to fixate on others' problems and much more difficult to look at your own head on.—Toby, age 19[a]

A lot of people say you need to forgive, but really that's a false start. You need acceptance, taking things as they were. Because nothing can make them undone, ever.

I had a lot of anger in me. When I felt like I wasn't getting what I need, I would get angry with people. And my communication skills weren't very good. This would all end in yelling and ugly fights. That's when I started meditation, because I realized that I couldn't change anyone else. I started calming down and just walking away. The more I calmed my mind the less I needed to yell.[7]

Recognition

The first step in the process of healing then becomes recognizing the impact of the sexual assault on the individual's views of the world and of one's self. This can be accomplished through personal examination of the assault and the impact of the assault. It may be important to seek support during this time as it can help you reach a better understanding of what has happened. Counseling is a good, safe place to start the healing process. It is important to find the right counselor, one with whom you have a connection and who has experience working with trauma victims.[8] Seeking support may also mean turning to friends or family. Support groups, either online or in person, are another great resource. Some also seek spiritual or religious support.[9]

Online support groups and resources like the Rape, Abuse and Incest National Network's online chat are great places to reach out for support.

In the following story, eighteen-year-old Meagan describes how she reached out to others for support during the healing process. She also talks about the challenges faced during this time:

I received therapy from several specialists and a general therapist. I went through group therapy and I read many books on what happened to me. I also started going back to church where I made many friends and the day I told them and my group leader was the most nerve-wracking of them all. I have never met a group of Christians so supportive in my life. They sat and cried with me as they all hugged me and told me how strong I was. I was so scared that they would shun me because I wasn't a virgin but they only showed me love and compassion.

The healing process was and still is very hard. I will have to go through it for the rest of my life. There will always be days harder than others but eventually they won't be so common. But I am prepared to deal with them for the rest of my life. Currently I am still having flashbacks and dealing with the fear and constant looking over my shoulder but I know that if it was to happen again that I would know how to protect myself. I would still survive in that situation because I'm still standing after all of this.[10]

This process of seeking help usually starts when an individual can no longer avoid the impact of the sexual assault, either because she no longer wishes to avoid it or because the interference with daily life has become so great that avoidance is no longer an option.[11] With the seeking of help will come a recognition of the damage from the assault and of the impact of negative self-beliefs. It may take an individual a long time after beginning the healing process before she is ready to delve into some of the deeper issues related to the assault, either alone or with the aid of a counselor.[12] It's important to remember that everyone heals at his or her own pace, and the trauma from sexual assault isn't something that can heal overnight.

Some survivors may delay dealing with recovery until some crisis forces them to recognize the impact the abuse has had on their life. The next survivor was molested as a child and then raped as a teenager. It took Laurie a long time to recognize the impact her abuse had both on herself and on those around her:

I was raised with an alcoholic father who was very verbally abusive. He would come home and yell and throw things. My mother would take me to hotels at night to try to get sleep for school. My brothers—he never physically abused myself or my mom, but he would my brothers. They would fight in the driveway. I remember a lot of blood and the cops being called. Cops told my mom if she didn't leave my dad, she would be dead. They divorced when I was ten; we up and left in the middle of the night. Somewhere in the midst of that we were staying at my uncle's, when I was about six. He started taking me downstairs in the middle of the night and sexually abusing me. This went on for about two years.

I spent most of my life trying to bury it and pretend it didn't happen. It wasn't like I forgot it and would have flashbacks—I remember it. I just pretended that it wasn't any big deal. This is what happened, kind of thing. Now my mom feels a lot of guilt because I didn't really come out and tell my family. A couple of years ago I ruined my marriage, and that's when I came out about it. That's when my mom and everyone learned about it.

I did all kinds of sports, I worked, I had good grades, but I was still a rebellious teenager. I did anything I could, drug wise. I just didn't really care about myself. I was a virgin. I had the same boyfriend for three years in high school, and I was still a virgin. Even though I was a rebellious teenager, I guess that was my way to protect myself. Until on my eighteenth birthday, four of my friends, we partied. I was with my friend and we were drinking. He slipped me roofies that night, and he raped me. I remember waking up next to my friend and taking a shower. The cops being called and being taken to the hospital, and they did a rape kit on me. And then meeting with the cops and having the cops showing me pictures of my friend, who I thought was my friend, of what he looked like after my friends had beaten him up. The cops said, "Oh, your friends took care of it. You don't want to go through all this." And they talked me out of pressing charges. I felt mortified, and ashamed, and dirty. I just didn't do anything or go anywhere for a few days. I regret not pressing charges. I don't know if he did it again. He could have just continued to get away with whatever; there's no way to tell if he did it again.

I was in high school at the time, so everyone knew when I went back to school. Everyone knew. And it was so hard. I could see how it looked, I was drinking, maybe I asked for it, maybe I caused it. I was a senior, and I could have graduated half a year early, but instead I graduated half a year late. My grades had slipped and everything. But I finally got back on track. I think I did more damage to myself than anyone else. I should have never been ashamed. I didn't ask for it. It wasn't my fault.

Over the next few years I did everything I could, apart from putting a gun to my head. I did a lot of drugs. I didn't care for myself or respect myself at all. Then I met my husband when I was twenty-one. We had a good marriage, but I was an abuse victim, a rape victim, and I grew up in an alcoholic house. I probably wasn't the best wife.

My husband walked out a few years ago. He just went to work and never came home. That's when I finally started fixing everything—I didn't drink every day, but when I drank it was a problem. When I drank, I didn't know how to stop. About two years ago I got sober. Then that's when I went to a survivor's retreat. I had to deal with what had been done to me. I couldn't run from it any more. I found that my passion was for youth, because I felt like my youth had been stolen from me. I don't want youth to feel like they can't stand up and say something. . . . I don't want that to happen to other people. I don't want them to hurt and feel like it's their fault. I felt so ashamed for so long. I didn't feel like anyone could understand me, or what had happened to me. Or could relate to me. Then all I did was blame myself. After the retreat, it just opened everything up.[13]

Common Therapies for Sexual Assault Victims

While many survivors of sexual assault choose not to seek formal services like counseling and therapy, these services can greatly improve the quality and the

Precious: Based on the Novel *Push* by Sapphire

Based on the novel *Push*, which was published in 1996, *Precious* is about a sixteen-year-old overweight teen named Claireece Precious who is being physically and emotionally abused by her mother and sexually abused by her father. She is also pregnant for the second time, both times by her father. She is illiterate and struggling. She is expelled from school for being pregnant and is sent to an alternative school where she finally learns to read. When her mother drops her newborn baby on purpose, Precious has finally had enough. With the help of a social worker and her teacher, Precious gets custody of her children and moves out on her own. She makes plans to get her GED and attend college. Will she succeed, with the odds so much against her? That is left unclear.

Director Lee Daniels read the book *Push* and felt a special connection to the story because he had been abused by his father when he was a child. Initially, when Daniels approached the author of *Push*, the author/poet Sapphire, she was unwilling to sell Daniels the rights. She had already turned down several other offers. After seeing other movies directed by Daniels, Sapphire agreed. The movie still did not have a studio backing it, and Daniels had to raise the nearly $10 million it took to film the movie. When it first showed at the Sundance Film Festival in 2009, it was extremely well received and won the Audience Award and the Grand Jury Prize for best drama. At this point, Tyler Perry and Oprah Winfrey stepped in to support the film, which led to it being picked up and distributed by Lionsgate Entertainment. Both Perry and Winfrey were physically and sexually abused as children and felt a strong connection with the film.

While some have criticized the film for negative portrayals of black characters and for reinforcing stereotypes about black people and black families, Daniels has defended the film, arguing that it portrays truths that make people uncomfortable, examining not only incest and child abuse, but also the intersection of race and poverty, compounded by a lack of education. It also shows a victim of sexual assault escaping an abusive home and beginning the process of recovery.[b]

speed of recovery and healing. There are many different treatment options available. These six are among the most common:

1. *Supportive counseling:* This form of therapy is the kind that is commonly offered in rape crisis centers. The victim is able to talk freely about the sexual assault, while the therapist actively listens and provides support and positive regard. It's argued that while this form of therapy may be beneficial immediately following a traumatic event, long-term psychological problems may need additional treatment to be resolved.[14]

2. *Stress inoculation therapy:* A cognitive behavior therapy, this type has been proven successful in treating rape victims who suffer from elevated levels of fear, stress, and anxiety, as well as victims who experience symptoms of PTSD. It is designed to help victims overcome their fear and work through any avoidance behaviors they may have developed as a response to trauma. The therapy consists of several steps. First is education. Fear is a normal response to a traumatic event like sexual assault. Understanding that, and understanding what may trigger fear and anxiety—things like places or smells associated with the assault— is the first step in overcoming those fears. Second, victims are guided through ways to control their reactions to these triggers. Cognitive techniques to control these fears can be used. Some of these techniques include guided self-talk, which is a way for survivors to talk themselves through difficult situations that may remind them of the assault; thought stopping, which is a way of training the mind to interrupt intrusive thoughts; and mental rehearsal, or imagining and visualizing an ideal reaction to such triggers. The final step in this kind of therapy is to face the things that trigger fear. Those participating in this type of therapy are encouraged to stop self-criticism and avoidance behaviors, as well as to reward themselves for progress made.[15]

3. *Prolonged exposure therapy:* Successful in addressing feelings of guilt and depression caused by trauma, as well as PTSD symptoms, prolonged exposure therapy is also a cognitive behavior therapy. The goal of this kind of therapy is to desensitize the victim to rape trauma by as much exposure to the experience as possible. Those being treated in this therapy will be asked to recount the sexual assault many times, and may even listen to audio recordings of the account to further increase exposure. A victim may be asked to revisit real-life situations that bring up memories of the sexual assault. This form of therapy is also known as "flooding."[16]

4. *Cognitive processing therapy:* Another form of cognitive behavior therapy, this approach focuses on challenging problematic beliefs that may have developed as a result of the sexual assault.[17] Clients are encouraged to con-

sider their belief systems, compare them to what beliefs they held prior to the sexual assault, and challenge these beliefs. Clients are also asked to write about the assault and read it to the therapist, the purpose of which is to identify "stuck points," or places where the victim is still struggling to process and cope.[18]

5. *Eye movement desensitization reprocessing (EMDR):* The purpose of EMDR is to help the trauma victim fully process the trauma. Clients are focused on internalizing the experience in healthy ways. The theory is that the memory of the event, and anything learned from the event, will remain, but the distress and trauma associated with it will be gone. Eye movements, which usually consist of following the therapist's finger from side to side, or other repetitive actions may be used to help in the processing of the trauma.[19] EMDR is considered by most to be questionable because it's unclear whether the eye movements contribute to the positive effects of the therapy, or if it's simply exposure from talking about the trauma that is beneficial.[20]

6. *Multiple-channel exposure therapy:* Often new treatments will be developed or adapted to meet needs as they are recognized. For example, Dr. Sherry Falsetti and colleagues developed multiple-channel exposure therapy to address PTSD and panic disorder. This treatment uses a combination of cognitive processing therapy and panic control treatments.[21] An initial study showed that this treatment was extremely effective at reducing both PTSD symptoms and panic attacks.[22]

Many states have programs to pay for services needed by victims of crime, including therapy needed by victims of sexual assault. If you are in need of therapy services, check to see what programs are available in your state to help pay for services. Some states may require the assault to be reported to the police before compensation is provided. The following story is from a survivor who used EMDR:

I had never heard of EMDR when my therapist proposed trying it with me. I was suffering from chronic PTSD related to a sexual assault when I was eighteen and an incidence of molestation when I was a preschooler. The main symptoms troubling me were intrusive thoughts and flashbacks. My therapist explained that EMDR would allow me to revisit these thoughts and memories in a safe environment, in order to help my brain integrate and stop wrestling with them.

We started with the traditional method of the therapist rhythmically moving her pointed fingers back and forth—almost like you could imagine a hypnotist doing. I was supposed to track the movements with my eyes, but it didn't work for me. I have dry, easily irritated eyes, and I kept rubbing at my contact lenses or blinking. Luckily, my therapist had an alternate system that worked just as well. I rested a small electronic device by me, and held onto smooth palm-sized pieces that vibrated alternately left-right, left-right, in that same rhythm.

My therapist let me lead, going through whichever memory or disturbing thought came up for me in the moment. For example, several times I processed specific scenes from the assault, but other times I worked with things like "feeling stupid" for placing myself in a vulnerable situation. Though I picked the content that spontaneously emerged, my therapist encouraged me to feel deeply in my body any of the emotions and physical sensations being elicited. I had problems specifically with dissociation, so I think my therapist was trying to counteract that, but I assume it may be a standard part of EMDR as well.

I only did about ten sessions of EMDR; I think the number of sessions needed varies widely for each person. My intrusive thoughts and flashbacks stopped, at least to the level where I now only have one very occasionally, and then only if a related trigger crops up unexpectedly. Before, my triggers had become broader and broader (i.e., almost all men), and I sometimes even had symptoms out of the blue. Though I completed my EMDR therapy, my therapist let me know that I can always come back if I need more sessions.[23]

For some, the process of telling the story of their sexual assault, either directly to another person or through writing, can be a very helpful step in the healing process. Many people keep their experience a secret and avoid disclosure. Telling the secret, giving voice to what is hidden, can be a very validating experience. It is important for this disclosure to be the choice of the individual and not something she or he is forced to do.[24] Story telling also gives survivors the opportunity to reframe the event. By examining the experience closely and giving words to it, they will be able to recognize their role in the events. The survivors will be able to recognize that it wasn't their fault, they are not to blame, and are not bad people because this happened to them.[25] The process of deliberately writing about a traumatic event has also shown to lead to better emotional and physical health, aiding in the individual's ability to cope with stress.[26]

There have also been some studies done to examine the effectiveness of alternative treatments. In a preliminary study, yoga was shown to reduce the severity of PTSD symptoms. It is also believed that yoga might be beneficial in helping to treat depression and stress after a sexual assault.[27] In addition, meditation appears to be an effective addition to traditional treatments in managing and reducing PTSD symptoms.[28] Studies have also shown that exercise is beneficial in helping adults, teens, and even children overcome PTSD symptoms, anxiety, and depression.[29] Of course, you should discuss both traditional treatments and alternative treatments with your therapist or psychiatrist.

Many survivors find a sense of meaning and purpose through activism. Volunteering to help other survivors as they work toward recovery and healing can bring peace and importance. Advocacy work is also a great way to aid others.[30] The last chapter of this work will discuss activism more fully.

Depending on the severity and duration of your depression or PTSD symptoms, your doctor or psychiatrist may prescribe medication to help you manage your symptoms. It's important to discuss possible side effects and alternatives before starting to take medication. However, in many cases the benefits of prescription medication outweigh potential side effects.[31]

For Destiny, counseling was key to breaking free from a cycle of negative self-thought and destructive behavior. Her story of recovery illustrates how many survivors reach an extreme low point before reaching out for help. Not only does she talk about the positive growth she experienced from counseling, but she also discusses constructive coping mechanisms, like journaling, that have replaced unhealthy behaviors. She also recounts her personal triumphs during recovery:

> At the beginning of the process, I dealt with my anger by lashing out and pushing people away. I cut off friendships with anyone I knew from the church I'd attended. I stopped spending time with my family. I shied away from family events, ignored calls/texts from family members and stayed home. After trying to reach me so many times, they stopped. So I picked fights with friends at school over small things. I shut down when they'd ask if something was wrong and rejected their invites to go out. After a while a few friends pulled back too, sad I'd become so negative. At that point, I thought about hurting myself . . . that was a really dark time. I felt alone, but I'd alienated myself out of anger and fear.
>
> After counseling, I've learned to deal with my issues in more constructive ways. When I'm upset, I handle my emotions by working out to blow off steam or writing in my diary. I make sure I get enough sleep, eat more and take care of health. I do my best not to take my frustrations out on others. If I'm feeling down, I reach out for help now so I'm not alone. There are still rough days when I'm down or angry, but I keep pushing forward. I'm mending relationships with my family and friends. They've been really supportive during this healing process. It feels great talking to them again. I've brought my grades up, passed the classes I'd failed previously and I'm finishing school this semester. I'll be graduating in December![32]

As hard as it is to heal after a sexual assault, it is possible to recover and to be happy again.

Scars

"Healing" from a sexual assault isn't always possible in the traditional sense, which is why many professionals use the word *recovery*. The assault or abuse will always be part of the survivor's story, like a scar. Recovery means coming to a place where the assault or abuse no longer interferes with day-to-day life.[33] It's important and helpful to reach a level of acceptance, both of the fact that the abuse occurred and of one's self. There will be a need for lifelong self-care and coping, but recovery is possible.[34]

Through the healing process, the sexual assault survivor experiences a transformation. Amazingly such a painful and traumatic experience can for some individuals also be a source of personal growth. The hard work of overcoming and working through the damage caused by an assault can lead to a deeper understanding and appreciation of oneself and the world. Healing brings with it a context for the assault. The sexual assault will always be a part of the survivor, but through healing, it will no longer be the defining element. The assault will be just one piece of what forms a whole, complete individual. With this transformation, the survivor will not only have better feelings about him- or herself, but will also be better able to connect and form relationships with others. After the healing process the survivor will then go on to have a more complete, fulfilling life.[35]

What Happens Next
by Colleen Clayton

Cassidy "Sid" Murphy goes on a ski trip with her two best friends and meets Dax, an older college guy who convinces Sid to go to a party. She wakes up the next morning with her sweater inside out and no memory of the night before. It soon becomes clear that she has been date raped.

Sid enters a downward spiral. She separates herself from friends and family, and becomes an obsessive night runner. She does start to develop a relationship with Corey, the high school slacker and rumored druggie. Slowly Sid starts to make progress toward healing and recovery as the novel comes to an end. This work is the author Colleen Clayton's debut novel.[c]

In the following story, nineteen-year-old Carolyn discusses both the recovery process and the scar that is left behind after healing from sexual assault. She also has some inspiring words to other survivors:

I spent a lot of time trying to "get over" my assault. So many times I sat in class, laid in bed, went out with friends, rung someone up at work, and I actively tried to push the memories out of my head. I imagine it now like a door into the darkest parts of my past. As I went about my day it would crack open and out would leak the little pieces, playing through my mind like a horrible movie. . . .

I've learned that the door will always find a way to open. A social worker that helped me along my healing journey described my life after the assault as a trauma spiral. The idea was that early in the healing process, you sit in the middle of this spiral and the assault is very close to you and feels like it is omnipresent in your life and thoughts. As time goes on and you further in your healing, more space is created for other thoughts and other focuses. It's never over, there is no end, no point where you're "healed," there's just more time and space between the lines of the spiral and the trauma won't seem so overwhelming.

Maybe this sounds a bit depressing, that you'll never get to a point in life where it won't matter anymore and your life can go back to the way it was before "it" happened. But I think that's a good thing. I would argue that the perseverance and the strength that it takes to survive each day after the assault is something to be immensely proud of. And I don't think we should ever be "over" that, or forget that. When we live our lives and inevitably that door starts to open, let's use it as an opportunity to remind ourselves of the incredible strengths we have because of our journey. Let's be proud of what we have faced and emerged from. So for other survivors I hope that you never "get over it." I hope that you never stop being proud of yourself for getting up today and taking a step forward in life. You are incredible. You are resilient. You deserve to be here. You deserve to smile. Be proud, stand tall, keep moving.[36]

ACTIVISM

W hether you are a survivor of sexual assault or just someone who is concerned about the current epidemic of sexual violence, it's natural to want to do something to help. The only way that laws will be reformed, campus disciplinary hearings will improve, or the culture of violence will change is through the activism of everyday people.

However, it's hard to know where to start. This chapter will examine some different kinds of activism and how to begin to make a difference.

Be Informed

Being informed on the issue and how pervasive it is in our society is an important first step. You can start by paying attention to your local news, as well as to national and international news. There are also many great resources online. Here are some websites with more information on sexual assault:

- *Childhelp:* www.childhelp.org. Childhelp has resources and information on child abuse, childhood sexual assault, and how to report it. It operates a 24/7 hotline that provides crisis counseling, information on how to report child abuse or neglect, information on the signs of abuse and neglect, and connection to local resources. The hotline number is 1-800-4-A-CHILD (1-800-422-4453).
- *Darkness to Light:* www.d2l.org. Darkness to Light provides information on childhood sexual assault. It also offers training on how to recognize the signs of childhood sexual assault and how to prevent abuse.
- *End Rape on Campus (EROC):* www.endrapeoncampus.org. EROC provides information and support to college students who have been sexually assaulted. The website provides information on the different laws that pertain to sexual assault on campus, including Title IX and the Clery Act. EROC also provides assistance in filing a Title IX complaint, as well as help in finding services.

- *Know Your IX:* www.knowyourix.org. This website provides information on Title IX and how colleges should respond to sexual assault. It also provides information on different forms of activism that students can pursue.
- *Love Is Respect:* www.loveisrespect.org. Information and resources pertaining to teen dating violence. The site also has a live 24/7 chat, a hotline at 1-866-331-9474, and a text message option. Text LOVEIS to 22522.
- *National Sexual Violence Resource Center:* www.nsvrc.org. This organization's website has a large collection of information on sexual assault, including legal information.
- *Not Alone:* www.notalone.gov. Not Alone is a government website dedicated to educating students about Title IX and sexual assault. The information on this site pertains to both colleges and universities, as well as to public schools from kindergarten on up. The site also has a list of other resources.
- *Rape, Assault and Incest National Network (RAINN):* www.rainn.org. This website has lots of information on sexual assault. It also has information in Spanish. At rainn.org/public-policy you can look up the laws in your state, as well as federal laws. This site is updated annually. RAINN also offers many volunteer opportunities, which will be discussed later in this chapter.
- *Stop It Now:* www.stopitnow.org. Provides information on the signs of child sexual abuse as well as prevention information. This organization also offers prevention training.
- *The US Department of Justice National Sex Offender Public Website:* www .nsopw.gov/en-US. On this website you can look to see if there are registered sex offenders in your area. Sometimes it's nice to know who is in the area you're walking or jogging in. However, not all predators are registered offenders.

These are just a few of the sources of information about sexual assault that are available. It's a good starting place for learning more about this topic.

Raise Awareness

After you've become more informed about this topic, the next way you can become involved in stopping sexual assault is by raising awareness. One of the reasons why rape culture is so predominant, why victims are blamed so much for their assaults, and why they blame themselves is because we don't talk about this problem. People aren't knowledgeable enough about what sexual assault is and what rape is. They don't know how to respond when someone confides that she

Missoula *by Jon Krakauer*

Investigative journalist Jon Krakauer explored the hundreds of sexual assaults reported in the college town of Missoula, Montana, between 2008 and 2012, and how these assaults were largely mishandled or ignored. He also examined how Missoula is not unique, but rather a typical example of how sexual assault is handled by colleges and police departments across the country. Krakauer follows the story of five victims of sexual assault and exposes how their cases were handled. Using descriptive narrative to bring startling statistics to life, this book has helped bring the reality of sexual assault on campus to light.[a]

or he has been assaulted. When individuals are assaulted, they don't always have the language to identify what has happened or the information to find the help needed. This is why sharing information about sexual assault, and the resources available, is so important.

Thanks to social media, sharing information with friends and family members is incredibly easy. You can simply post links to interesting articles or news stories

PACT5

PACT5 is a partnership between the documentary film departments from five universities: Rowan University, California State University at Northridge, Western Colorado University, Northern Illinois University, and Framingham University. The goal of PACT5 is to use student-created documentaries to educate students about sexual assault, and ultimately to prevent sexual assault on campus. The schools plan to use the documentaries in a variety of ways to educate and raise awareness. Some of the films can be viewed on the PACT5 website at www.pact5.org/pact5-documentaries. PACT5 is looking for other college film departments to join them in seeking to end sexual violence.[b]

or links to websites that provide more information. Posting some of the more startling statistics about sexual assault can catch a reader's attention, prompting him or her to click on the link you provide to learn more.

There are also print materials available that you can share. The Rape, Abuse and Incest National Network offers some print materials for free at www.rainn .org.

For survivors, finding ways to share their stories to help others and to raise awareness can be very meaningful, and can help with the healing/recovery process. In the following stories, Jannina and Tiffany talk about ways they have found to share their stories with others; first, Jannina, age twenty-three:

> I went to the police and to lawyers trying to report the crime, to seek justice, and after months of uncomfortable interviews, questioning, and phone calls, I was told nothing could be done because of the laws in New York and the time elapsed and because of my lapse in memory. . . .
>
> This newspaper was putting together a book that would be titled "The Survivors Project" that would collect essays of survivors who wanted to share their stories. These were essays of hurt, of pain, but ultimately essays of hope, of miraculous forgiveness, and of brighter futures. I got involved in this project and in doing so, began to speak out more at home about sexual abuse and the need for awareness and prevention programs. As I began to share my story with my family, they began to share their stories with me. Slowly, little by little, story after story of rape, of childhood molestation, of sexual violence began to come into the light. Generations of silence began to break, and though the news was absolutely horrifying, freedom began to saturate myself and my family. There are thirty-three people in the three generations that make up my generation through my grandmother's generation. Of these thirty-three people, fourteen people have been either raped, sexually molested, or forced under sexual violence. That is forty-two percent of the people in my family's past three generations and that is only the stories I know about. This shocked me, hurt me, angered me, and ultimately made me more passionate about becoming an advocate for the cause, and to speak out.[1]

Tiffany decided to write a book and craft a career to help others:

> Seven years later, I've written and published my book, *The Power of Adversity: A Guide to Finding Your Greatest Gift in Life* where I talk about my experience and share the lessons that I have learned in overcoming adversity and designing a meaningful life. This book is an Amazon best-

seller and I've shared this message with hundreds of readers. Writing has always been therapeutic, especially when writing this book. Occasionally, I experience triggers but because I've seen a therapist, have done a lot of inner development and have a supportive husband, I know how to better handle these triggers. I'm in a much better place in my life. I believe everything happens for a reason and my adversity at the age of eighteen was a blessing in disguise. I would not be the woman I am today if it weren't for the lessons that I learned with my adversity. Because of my adversity, I have found my calling in life. I am now the owner of a lifestyle coaching firm where I work with women on overcoming adversity and designing a meaningful life. I'm a motivational speaker, life coach, and author.[2]

Speak Up: Bystander Intervention

Constantly we hear the refrain "If you see something, say something." The same is true of sexual assault and victim blaming.

When someone says something that you know is wrong, speak up, and provide accurate information. For example, if you hear someone describe a rape victim as "asking for it," you can say this is victim blaming. Are murder victims or mugging victims "asking for it"?

Sometimes people will even brag about a sexual assault. Typically guys, but occasionally girls, will tell friends how they pressured their significant other into sex or used alcohol or drugs to initiate sex. When those friends remain silent, it is assumed that they support this behavior. This normalizes sexual assault and strengthens the rape culture we live in. Being silent during rape jokes or bragging sessions is supporting rape and rape culture. Speaking out, even when it is uncomfortable, can break a pattern of abuse and be the starting point of healthier relationships and sexual interactions.[3]

On college campuses, studies have shown that a small percentage of men are committing the majority of sexual assaults. Often there are witnesses to the assaults, and the witnesses do nothing. Because of this, a number of colleges have started conducting bystander training to help students recognize when a sexual assault is about to occur and then intervene.[4]

For teens and young adults, peer pressure and being socially accepted are very important, so bystander intervention can have a very powerful impact. Not only can it prevent an assault from taking place, but it can change the mind-set of the group and destroy tolerance for predatory behavior.[5]

Intervention as a bystander can have a direct or indirect approach. In a direct approach, someone sees a problem and actively steps in to stop it. For example,

Being a good friend to someone who has been sexually assaulted is one of the best ways to help combat sexual assault.

say you notice a guy at a party giving a girl drink after drink. Then you see him trying to lead her into a private area when she is clearly too impaired to consent. Direct intervention would be to step in and say the girl's ride is waiting outside or something else to get her out of danger. Indirect intervention would be to call the police.[6]

When intervening as a bystander you have to keep in mind your own personal safety. Things can escalate quickly. Whenever possible, get a few other people to help you intervene.

When the problem you are facing is one of long-term abuse, there are several things you also need to consider. In a case of teen dating violence, for example, you may want to draw up a plan before stepping in. Should you enlist the help of a parent, teacher, or school administrator? Does the person realize that she is in an abusive relationship? Consider carefully how you can bring this topic up without offending or alienating your friend. In a case of childhood sexual assault, the best intervention is reporting the abuse immediately. Since you may not know what is going on inside the child's home, a safe first step would be to notify law enforcement or your local child protective services. You can make a report anonymously. While everything may be just fine inside the child's home, it is better to err on the side of caution when you suspect child sexual abuse.[7]

There are many resources available to learn more about bystander intervention. A good place to start is the Step Up! program at www.stepupprogram.org. Another great resource is One Student at www.onestudent.org.

A great resource for men who are interested in ending sexual assault and gender-based violence is White Ribbon at www.whiteribbon.ca. This website offers direct and detailed suggestions on how men can help the fight against the sexual assault crisis.

Pain to Purpose: An Interview with an Employee at SAVAS

I parked my car next to a blue station wagon. It's early, and as I climb out of my vehicle, I notice a woman sleeping in the station wagon's driver's seat, a plaid comforter over her.

I walk up to SAVAS, the rape crisis center that serves all of Prince William County in northern Virginia. SAVAS stands for Sexual Assault and Victims Advocacy Service; the group has been part of the community for over thirty years. Like many crisis centers, it offers advocates to accompany victims to the hospital, the police station, even to court. This center also runs its own twenty-four-hour hotline and offers services in Spanish. I ask for Anita at the counter, with whom I have been exchanging emails, and then wait.

A few minutes later, a smiling woman approaches me and leads me down a long hall.

"This is where we bring our teen groups," she says.

Two long tables have been placed side by side, making a square. Stools surround the tables, and the tabletops are covered in large sheets of paper. Cans of markers sit at intervals. Morning light fills the space, filtering in from high windows. The walls are lined with masks, white masks that have been painted, most split vertically to show two different faces.

"We have the teens paint those," she says, noticing where my eyes have wandered. "One side represents what they show the world, the other what they really feel." The masks are haunting; some could be from horror movies.

"What brought you to this line of work?" I ask.

"I'm a survivor. I call it from pain to purpose. I went through a lot of self-destructive behaviors before I really started healing. I was molested from the age of seven until I was fourteen and that's around the time I started drinking and drugging, and I did that until I was well into my twenties. And that was my way of coping. I ran, I left the area, I moved across the country three times, thinking I'll just visit places. I was raped in my apartment when I was twenty. Then I met my husband, and had my daughter, and I thought okay. It's time to get real. It's time to stop running. I started reading. I had read as a child; it was a huge coping mechanism. Books were safe, books were my comfort. So when I started reading, I started learning and I wanted to know why. Then my daughter was raped when she was in college. That was when I was like okay, what are you trying to tell me? That's when I found SAVAS and I started volunteering. There's a lot of us out there."

"You say you were asking why. Did you ever find an answer?"

"This happens in secret. We see a lot of incest here, it's a stepfather or uncle or someone. Or there are women who come, and it happened in their childhood, like me. And the pain comes from the shame of this secret they carry. To me the antidote comes in opening the curtains and airing it out. It's not a secret; it's nothing to be ashamed of. We talk about it, and talk about it, and talk about it. With my kids in my family we talk about stuff. That's what drove me crazy as a child is what we didn't talk about, the secrets.

"I know when I found SAVAS it was the first time in my life it was such a relief because it's a place where we talk about it. We all talk about our stuff. All those years I was reading and thought I was healing it was still my big secret. I remember walking places and thinking if people only knew. I felt very disconnected because I didn't tell people what was behind the mask. That's why we do masks. They're mostly done by kids," she gestures again to the masks on the wall before continuing. "I remember sitting in school with all these people around thinking if they only knew what was really behind the mask. So some of them are what's behind the mask and what they show the world. I feel that the goal is to make it not so different, that the more they heal the less different the two sides are. . . . It's a comfort and a healing thing to find someone who gets it. Therapists often aren't comfortable with this, so people think therapy isn't for them, but they just haven't found the right one. A lot of people just need to be heard. They just need to know they aren't crazy, they aren't going to be looked at like they're a freak. It's normalizing it."

"Is that your hope in your work here?"

"With the teens my hope is that we can intervene now so they don't carry that weight with them. It's a journey. It's something that we manage. SAVAS is a wonderful place because we help each other. The art becomes a way to vocalize something you don't even know the words for." She pulls a sketch book from one of the bookcases and hands it to me. Inside it is filled with paintings, collages, and poetry.

"One of the girls who came here made this. It's her healing journey. When she was done with it, she left it here for other survivors to see."

Each page of the thick book is painstakingly detailed, and every inch of every page has been filled. This wasn't the work of weeks or months; it looks to have taken years.

"I don't take it lightly that many times people are sharing something they've never shared before. It's humbling, and I don't take that lightly. That they sit here and share with me things that are so profoundly painful and that they've kept secret for so long." She goes to another shelf and lifts an oversized black skull with white words written all over it. "This one girl, she doesn't say a word about what she's been through, she doesn't want to talk about it at all, but then one day she brought me this." The words, all caps, look stark and accusing against the black paint. CUT. RIP. HURT. BLEED. SILENT. DEATH. I can't take my eyes off the words, even as Anita puts the skull away.

"I learn from them," she says, looking around the room of books and masks. "They learn from me, I learn from them. The more we talk about it, the more it's put out there. I feel it is the only antidote to these horrific things."

Finally, she pulls a few small boxes from another shelf. The boxes are painted with intricate designs, bright and cheerful. She opens one, and the design is continued on the inside, only darker and sharper. "We do these boxes, because it never goes away. But one day you can put it in a box, and just every now and then pull it out and look at it. This is a part of you; it's not all of you."

I pack up my bag and thank her. As I move toward the door, she asks if she can hug me. We hug, and I feel grateful to be part of her story.[c]

Volunteer

Another way to get involved is to volunteer. The Rape, Abuse and Incest National Network keeps an up-to-date list of local sexual assault crisis centers and shelters, many of which rely on local volunteers. RAINN also staffs the National Sexual Assault Hotline with volunteers. You can visit its website at www.rainn.org.

Here are two survivors talking about the impact volunteering had on their recovery. This first survivor, Becky, was nineteen when she was abducted and raped when leaving her job. She was left abandoned in a junk yard. Like many survivors, it took her years to start to heal:

Twenty-four years of silence later, I couldn't sleep. One night I sat at the computer and googled the one word I wasn't able to utter out loud for twenty-four years . . . rape . . . I hit search. It almost felt like I had said the word out loud . . . I began to read . . . I saw words and descriptions that spoke to me . . . flashbacks, triggers, silence, shame, guilt . . . I read survivors' stories and I began to cry deeply for the first time. I saw myself in these survivors. I realized that I wasn't alone in this. I felt validated. It was okay to feel shattered. I felt a great relief for the first time that night. I read more and more over the next weeks and months and realized that being okay again was possible. Most importantly I felt hope. I began reaching out to my family and a few trusted friends. It took time but I continued to share my story with others and every time I did, it became a little easier. I stopped worrying about hurting others with my story. I stopped protecting them and started fighting for myself. Most people were incredibly supportive. It was taking less and less of my energy to live with my trauma, and I was able to put more energy into living my life. I stopped blaming myself for not fighting back. I no longer hated that nineteen-year-old girl.

I found RAINN'S website and read about their new online hotline. I thought about how my own journey would have been different if I had had an anonymous resource to reach out to. I became a volunteer for their new online hotline. Over the next three years, I took over a thousand calls to the hotline. My work with RAINN was helping me to heal. I began to feel whole again. After all those years, it wasn't too late!

The thirtieth anniversary of my assault was last December 15th. That day is still a significant day for me, but it no longer feels sad. I no longer dread the anniversary. It is no longer a day I simply have to survive. I acknowledge what happened to me because it was big. It was life altering. But, now, I celebrate life that day. I celebrate my life. I celebrate the strength and the courage of all of us survivors out there. I no longer wish for my life to go back to before, I don't remember what life was like before the rape, but the best part is, it doesn't matter anymore. I am no longer angry at the girl I was back then. Instead I am amazed at her bravery and will to live.

My rape does not define me. I claimed my life back when I began speaking about what happened to me. I met other survivors both male and female and realized there is great healing power in sharing our stories. . . .

We need to stop being silent about sexual assault just because it is uncomfortable to talk about. Rape is a crime of violence. Be a safe place for someone to reach out to. Be someone's strength. Be someone's support. If you know someone who is struggling right now, ask them if they are okay. Don't be afraid to talk to them. Tell them they are brave, tell them they are strong. Tell them that what happened was not their fault and they don't need to go through this alone. Fight beside them and if they can't fight, fight for them! They may not want to talk about it just then, but you've let them know, you care. You may not realize how important that is to them but it is.[8]

In the next story, twenty-four-year-old Taysa talks about her work on her college campus and as a facilitator at a shelter:

The healing process has been incredibly hard. I am in a much better place now, but I still struggle on a daily basis. I have seen multiple therapists over the years and all have helped, but I still go through bouts of depression. In these moments I try to look outside of myself and accept the help from family and friends.

After starting college I became trained in advocacy towards sexual and domestic violence. I began facilitating support groups for victims of domestic violence at a local shelter. I became the leader of a few on-campus groups aimed at raising awareness around the issues. These experiences greatly aided in my recovery. They gave purpose to the painful memories.[9]

Advocate for Legal Change

One of the many problems related to sexual assault is the way that sexual assaults are handled when they are reported. Often officials like police and campus security who are taking reports on sexual assaults aren't trained to know how to interact with victims in a way that doesn't traumatize them more. Campus policies or state laws may not be up to date with current research or with the needs of the victims. Nationwide over half the states have statutes of limitations on filing charges for rape or sexual assault, some of which are as short as three years.[10]

We can all push for positive change to help survivors of sexual assault.

Because of the traumatic nature of sexual assault, not all victims are ready to report an assault that soon.

But changes are starting to be made, and these changes are being made because of people who are advocating for change. Often laws and policies are just outdated and have never been updated to meet current needs. The only way they will be updated is if there are people who are pushing lawmakers and campus presidents to implement more victim-friendly policies and laws.

For example, Mel Townsend was raped in 2008, when she was a sophomore in college. As the years passed with no leads on her rapist, she became aware that in Kansas, where she was living, the statute of limitations was only five years. She lobbied her state legislators, and in March 2013 the statute of limitations was eliminated for all rape cases.[11]

In 2012, the FBI finally updated their eighty-five-year-old definition of rape as being "carnal knowledge of a female forcibly and against her will." This definition completely excludes men as potential victims, and it doesn't account for other sexual acts like sodomy, which are generally viewed as rape. It also doesn't take into account assaults that do not involve force, such as when the victim is incapacitated. This definition has contributed to misleading statistics of rape in the United States. The change came after more than a decade of pressure and advocacy from over ninety organizations such as the Women's Law Project.[12]

Another major problem facing the handling of rape cases is the overwhelming number of untested rape kits. While estimates vary as to exactly how many kits are untested, most agree that there are hundreds of thousands, some of them dating back decades.[13] The US Department of Justice estimates the number of untested kits to be about 400,000.[14] How important is the DNA evidence in a rape kit to seeking justice? Nationwide, arrests are made in about 24 percent of the rape cases that are reported to the police. In New York City, where every rape kit is tested, the arrest rate is 74 percent for rape cases.[15]

Thanks to growing awareness and public pressure, many states are beginning to take measures to address the rape kit backlog. In 2009 in Detroit, it was uncovered that eleven thousand untested kits were just sitting in a warehouse. To deal with this backlog, the Wayne County prosecutor's office partnered with UPS to create a tracking system for rape crisis kits. The tracking system was launched in January 2015, and by June 2015, about ten thousand of the kits from that warehouse had been tested. As a result of those tested kits, 326 suspected serial sex offenders were identified in thirty-two states. In that same time frame, there had been eighteen convictions from the DNA evidence in those kits.[16]

The first step to advocating for change is to know the laws in your state and what the problems are. RAINN has a database of state laws that can be found at www.rainn.org/public-policy.[17] The information available there for each state includes the statute of limitations for that state, if HIV/AIDS testing is required of the rapist, and if rapists have parental rights over a child that is a result of rape.

RAINN also has a page that gives simple, easy-to-follow steps for contacting your representative to lobby for laws to help assault victims. You can find the RAINN Action Center at www.rainn.org/public-policy/rainn-action-center.

You can also visit the Rape Kit Action Project at www.everykitcounts.org to learn more about what can be done about the rape kit backlog. The Rape Kit Action Project is working on a state-by-state basis to push for legislation to set policies in place to address the backlog. Learn what the backlog is in your state and if there's a policy in place to address it. If there's not, lobby for change.

Lobbying for change on a college campus is similar to lobbying for law changes. First, learn what the policy on your campus is and what resources are available. A good campus policy combines prevention efforts such as education and bystander training with accessible reporting resources. Twenty-four-hour emergency services and crisis intervention should be available to students, as well as long-term counseling. SAFER, at www.safercampus.org, has information on how to advocate for better campus policies, and the site also provides detailed guidelines on what makes a good campus sexual assault policy at www.safercampus.org/policy.

Personal stories are very powerful and can be a great aid in influencing law makers, school officials, and even police departments to make positive changes in the way that sexual assault is treated. The following is a story from Laurie, a survivor who joined a survivor advocacy group to petition the state of Georgia to pass a law to make it easier for victims of child sexual abuse to get the information they need to pursue a court case, and to extend the statute of limitations in some situations:

> I went downtown to the capital to protest, to help pass HB 17, the Hidden Predator Act for Georgia, to extend the reporting rights of child abuse victims. I helped push that with Voice Today. I helped lobby for that to pass, I shared my story. It was very empowering, I feel like I have a voice, I don't have to feel ashamed or dirty any more. This stuff happens way too often not to talk about it.[18]

It Matters

The actions of one individual, or those of a small group of individuals, may not seem like a lot, but they can make a big difference. Whether it involves raising awareness among friends on Facebook, volunteering at a crisis center, or moving for law changes in your state, your actions can make a difference in how sexual assault is viewed and in how it is handled, making the world a better place for survivors of sexual assault.

Glossary

acquaintance rape: when the perpetrator initiates a relationship or friendship with the victim prior to the assault; may involve drugs or alcohol.

advocate: usually a volunteer at a rape crisis center; person who offers emotional support and assistance to the victim. An advocate can accompany a victim of sexual assault to the hospital, to the police station, and even to court.

blitz sexual assault: sudden, violent assault by a stranger, usually in a public place.

bystander intervention: in a sexual assault context, when a bystander sees someone trying to initiate sex with someone who does not consent, usually someone who is intoxicated or incapacitated. Bystander intervention could be direct action or it could be indirect, like calling the police or getting someone else to step in.

campus assault: term used to denote assault involving college students.

child sexual assault or child sexual abuse: when the victim of sexual assault is a child.

coercion: pressure to have sex or perform sexual acts, including emotional manipulation.

consent: agreement to engage in sexual acts. It cannot be given by a person who is intoxicated or incapacitated, nor can it be given by a person under the legal age to give consent. Legal age varies by state.

contact sexual assault: when the perpetrator is a stranger and flirts or talks to the victim before assaulting him or her.

date rape: when the perpetrator initiates a relationship or friendship with the victim prior to the assault; may involve drugs or alcohol.

explicit knowledge: what a person consciously knows; these beliefs may be in conflict with subconscious or implicit knowledge.

grooming: the process used by a sexual predator to initiate a sexual relationship. This is used to initiate child sexual abuse and to keep it secret. It is also used to seduce teens and young adults into sex trafficking and sexual slavery.

home invasion assault: assault by a stranger who has broken into the victim's home.

human trafficking: the forced labor, sexual enslavement, or commercial sexual exploitation of people.

implicit knowledge: subconscious beliefs a person may not be aware of. These beliefs may be in conflict with explicit or conscious knowledge.

incest: sexual relationships between family members.

intimate partner sexual assault: sexual assault that happens in a relationship.

intimate partner violence: abuse in a relationship, including but not limited to sexual abuse.

just world belief: the belief that the world is fair and that if something bad happens to a person, it's because the person has done something to cause it or deserve it.

military sexual assault or military sexual trauma: sexual assault in the military; includes all branches of the armed forces.

normalize: sexual predators, especially those who prey on children, will try to convince victims that the sexual abuse is normal, or an expression of love; also refers to advocates, therapists, and others reassuring a survivor that the feelings he/she may have after an assault are normal.

pedophile: someone who is sexually attracted to children.

prevention training: a controversial training that focuses on teaching young women risk-reduction behavior and self-defense.

prison rape: sexual assault of inmates. The perpetrator could be another inmate, a prison guard, or other prison staff.

rape crisis center: local community centers with volunteers, advocates, and resources for survivors of sexual assault.

rape culture: messages imbedded in a culture that support or promote rape and sexual violence.

rape kit: a kit used in a hospital to gather DNA evidence after a sexual assault.

rape myth: a false belief about rape, such as women lie about being raped or rapists are all strangers hiding in dark alleys.

rape script: a belief about how a rape occurs or the story of a rape. For many people, a rape script is a blitz rape with a stranger attacking a victim in a public place at night, usually with a weapon. Rape script is what a person thinks a rape looks like.

sexual assault: any form of unwanted sexual contact; any sexual contact without express consent.

stranger assault: when the perpetrator of sexual assault is not known to the victim.

teen dating violence: a range of abusive behaviors in teen relationships, including emotional, physical, and sexual abuse, as well as cyberbullying.

victim blaming: when the victim is blamed for her assault because of what she wore, where she went, who she was with, whether she drank, how late she was out. Victim blaming is anything that shifts responsibility for the assault from the rapist to the victim.

Notes

Chapter 1

1. Rape, Abuse and Incest National Network, "Sexual Assault," www.rainn.org/get-information/types-of-sexual-assault/sexual-assault. Accessed December 26, 2015.
2. Rape, Abuse and Incest National Network, "Sexual Assault."
3. Rape, Abuse and Incest National Network, "The Offenders," www.rainn.org/get-information/statistics/sexual-assault-offenders. Accessed December 26, 2015.
4. Rape, Abuse and Incest National Network, "How Often Does Sexual Assault Occur?" www.rainn.org/get-information/statistics/frequency-of-sexual-assault. Accessed December 26, 2015.
5. Rape, Abuse and Incest National Network, "Reporting Rates," www.rainn.org/get-information/statistics/reporting-rates. Accessed December 26, 2015.
6. Melanie Eversley, "System Tackles Backlog of Rape Evidence, *USA Today*, June 8, 2015, 5A.
7. Destiny, personal narrative, received November 11, 2015.
8. Rape, Abuse and Incest National Network, "Who are the Victims?" www.rainn.org/get-information/statistics/sexual-assault-victims. Accessed December 26, 2015.
9. University of Michigan, "Sexual Assault and Women of Color," www.sapac.umich.edu/article/57. Accessed December 26, 2015.
10. Women of Color Network, "Sexual Violence Facts," www.doj.state.or.us/victims/pdf/women_of_color_network_facts_sexual_violence_2006.pdf. Accessed December 26, 2015.
11. Women of Color Network, "Sexual Violence Facts."
12. Women of Color Network, "Sexual Violence Facts."
13. Women of Color Network, "Sexual Violence Facts."
14. "The Violence Against Women Act—Title IX: Safety for Indian Women," *Tribal Court Clearing House*, www.tribal-institute.org/lists/title_ix.htm. Accessed March 19, 2016.
15. Diana Ozemebhoya Eromosele, "The Diverse Ways They Each Coped with Child Abuse," *Root*, April 19, 2014, www.theroot.com/articles/history/2014/04/famous_black_men_who_were_sexually_abused_as_kids_and_why_some_didn_t_know.html. Accessed March 21, 2016.
16. Lauren Paulk, "Sexual Assault in the LGBT Community," National Center for Lesbian Rights, April 30, 2014, www.nclrights.org/sexual-assault-in-the-lgbt-community. Accessed December 27, 2015.
17. National Sexual Violence Resource Center, "Sexual Violence and Individuals Who Identify as LGBTQ," www.nsvrc.org/sites/default/files/Publications_NSVRC_Research-Brief_Sexual-Violence-LGBTQ.pdf. Accessed December 27, 2015.
18. Paulk, "Sexual Assault in the LGBT Community."
19. National Sexual Violence Resource Center, "Sexual Violence and Individuals Who Identify as LGBTQ."
20. Jannina, personal narrative, received July 23, 2015, signed permission form to publish.

21. Rape, Abuse and Incest National Network, "Sexual Assault."

22. Rape, Abuse and Incest National Network, "Child Sexual Abuse," www.rainn.org/get -information/types-of-sexual-assault/child-sexual-abuse. Accessed December 27, 2015.

23. David G. Curtis, "Perspectives on Acquaintance Rape," American Academy of Experts in Traumatic Stress, www.aaets.org/article13.htm. Accessed December 27, 2015.

24. National Sexual Violence Resource Center, "What Is Campus Sexual Violence?" www .nsvrc.org/publications/nsvrc-publications-sexual-assault-awareness-month-fact-sheets/ saam-2015-what-campus. Accessed December 27, 2015.

25. Rape, Abuse and Incest National Network, "Intimate Partner Sexual Violence," www.rainn. org/get-information/types-of-sexual-assault/partner-rape. Accessed December 27, 2015.

26. NORC at the University of Chicago, "Preliminary Results in Landmark National Survey on Teen Dating Violence Finds Disturbingly High Rates of Victimization and Perpetra- tion by Both Girls and Boys," www.norc.org/NewsEventsPublications/PressReleases/Pages/ preliminary-results-in-landmark-national-survey-on-teen-dating-violence-finds-disturbingly -high-rates-of-victimization.aspx. Accessed December 27, 2015.

27. National Sexual Violence Resource Center, "Sexual Assault and Sexual Harassment in the U.S. Military Highlights from the 2014 RAND Military Workplace Study," www.nsvrc.org/ publications/research-briefs/sexual-assault-and-sexual-harassment-us-military-highlights -2014-rand. Accessed December 27, 2015.

28. Polaris, "Sex Trafficking," www.polarisproject.org/sex-trafficking. Accessed December 27, 2015.

29. Rape, Abuse and Incest National Network, "Prisoner Rape," www.rainn.org/get-informa- tion/types-of-sexual-assault/prison-rape. Accessed December 27, 2015.

30. Laura, age twenty-six, personal narrative, previously published in *Salon*, received August 20, 2015.

31. Rape, Abuse and Incest National Network, "Effects of Sexual Assault," www.rainn.org/get- information/effects-of-sexual-assault. Accessed December 27, 2015.

32. Rebecca M. Hayes, Katherine Lorenz, and Kristin A. Bell, "Victim Blaming Others: Rape Myth Acceptance and the Just World Belief," *Feminist Criminology* 8, no. 3 (2013): 202–220.

33. Rape, Abuse and Incest National Network, "After an Assault," www.rainn.org/get-informa- tion/sexual-assault-recovery/tips-for-after-an-attack. Accessed December 27, 2015.

34. Rape, Abuse and Incest National Network, "Aftermath of Sexual Assault," www.rainn.org/ get-information/aftermath-of-sexual-assault. Accessed December 27, 2015.

35. Rape, Abuse and Incest National Network, "What Is a Rape Kit?" www.rainn.org/get -information/sexual-assault-recovery/rape-kit. Accessed March 21, 2016.

36. Rape, Abuse and Incest National Network, "Self-Care after Trauma," www.rainn.org/get -information/sexual-assault-recovery/self-care-for-survivors. Accessed December 27, 2015.

37. Rape, Abuse and Incest National Network, "Title IX," www.rainn.org/get-info/legal -information/federal-laws/TitleIX. Accessed December 28, 2015.

38. Rape, Abuse and Incest National Network, "Victims of Crime Act," www.rainn.org/get-info/ legal-information/federal-laws/VOCA. Accessed December 28, 2015.

39. Rape, Abuse and Incest National Network, "Clery Act," www.rainn.org/get-info/legal -information/federal-laws/Clery-Act. Accessed December 27, 2015.

40. Rape, Abuse and Incest National Network, "Prisoner Rape."

41. Rape, Abuse and Incest National Network, "Debbie Smith Act," www.rainn.org/get-info/ legal-information/federal-laws/Debbie-Smith-Act. Accessed December 27, 2015.

42. Rape, Abuse and Incest National Network, "Campus SaVE Act," www.rainn.org/get-info/legal-information/federal-laws/Campus-SaVE-Act. Accessed December 27, 2015.

43. Rape, Abuse and Incest National Network, "SAFER Act," www.rainn.org/get-info/legal-information/federal-laws/SAFER-Act. Accessed December 27, 2015.

44. National Network to End Domestic Violence, "Violence Against Women Act," www.nnedv.org/policy/issues/vawa.html. Accessed December 28, 2015.

45 Rape, Abuse and Incest National Network, "Public Policy," www.rainn.org/public-policy. Accessed December 28, 2015.

---

a. Greg Logsted, *Something Happened* (New York: Simon Pulse, 2008).

b. Eugene Volokh, "Statutory Rape Laws and Ages of Consent in the US," *Washington Post*, May 1, 2015, www.washingtonpost.com/news/volokh-conspiracy/wp/2015/05/01/statutory-rape-laws-in-the-u-s/. Accessed March 19, 2016.

c. Sutter Health, "Consent and Consensual Sex," www.pamf.org/teen/abc/sex/consent.html. Accessed January 1, 2016.

d. Ashley Anderson and Elizabeth Deutsch, "Stop Assaults on Military Campuses," *New York Times*, May 12, 2015, A23.

e. Anderson and Deutsch, "Stop Assaults on Military Campuses," A23.

f. Kevin Johnson, "105 Kids Rescued from Prostitution Rings; 159 Arrested," *USA Today*, July 30, 2013, www.usatoday.com/story/news/nation/2013/07/29/fbi-arrest-child-prostitution-ring-rescue/2595725. Accessed March 21, 2016.

g. Brett M Decker, "America's Prisons Remain Rife with Rape," *Northwestern*, July 26, 2015, www.thenorthwestern.com/story/opinion/columnists/2015/07/26/americas-prisons-remain-rife-rape/30699787. Accessed March 21, 2016.

h. Christa Desir, *Fault Line* (New York: Simon Pulse, 2013).

i. *Tapestries of Hope*, "About the Movie," www.tapestriesofhope.com/about-the-movie/. Accessed January 1, 2016.

Chapter 2

1. Kyle Lierman, "It's on Us, a Growing Movement to End Campus Sexual Assault," *White House Blog*, September 24, 2014, www.whitehouse.gov/blog/2014/09/24/its-us-growing-movement-end-campus-sexual-assault. Accessed February 9, 2015.

2. Eliza Gray, "Taking Assault Seriously: Colleges Ramp Up Efforts to Make Students Safer," *Time*, September 1, 2014, 14.

3. Rape, Abuse and Incest National Network, "Reporting Rates," www.rainn.org/get-information/statistics/reporting-rates. Accessed February 9, 2015.

4. TeensHealth, "Date Rape," kidshealth.org/en/teens/date-rape.html?WT.ac=ctg#catproblems. Accessed February 9, 2015.

5. Barbara Mantel, "Campus Sexual Assault," *CQ Researcher* 24, no. 39 (October 31, 2014): 913–936.

6. Meagan, personal narrative, received December 10, 2015.

7. Mantel, "Campus Sexual Assault," 913–936.

8. Katha Pollitt, "Yes to 'Yes Means Yes,'" *Nation*, October 27, 2014, 6–7.

9. Susan A. Basow and Alexandra Minier, "'You Owe Me': Effects of Date Cost, Who Pays, Participant Gender, and Rape Myth Beliefs on Perceptions of Rape," *Journal of Interpersonal Violence* 26, no. 3 (February 2011): 479–497.

10. Taysa, personal narrative, received December 3, 2015.

11. Michelle Goldberg, "Campus Rape Crisis," *Nation*, June 23/30, 2014, 12–16.

12. Gray, "Taking Assault Seriously," 14.

13. Mantel, "Campus Sexual Assault," 913–936.

14. Charlene Y. Senn, Misha Eliasziw, Paula C. Barata, Wilfreda E. Thurston, Ian Newby-Clark, H. L. Radtke, and Karen L. Hobden, "Efficacy of a Sexual Assault Resistance Program for University Women," *New England Journal of Medicine* 372, no. 24 (June 11, 2015): 2326–2335.

15. Jan Hoffman, "College Rape Prevention Program Proves a Rare Success," *New York Times*, June 10, 2015, A15.

16. The Editorial Board, "To Prevent Sexual Assault, Start Early," *New York Times*, July 14, 2015, A20.

17. Lierman, "It's on Us."

18. Mantel, "Campus Sexual Assault," 913–936.

19. Mantel, "Campus Sexual Assault," 913–936.

20. Susanne Craig and Jesse McKinley, "New York's Lawmakers Agree on Campus Assault Laws," *New York Times*, June 16, 2015, www.nytimes.com/2015/06/17/nyregion/new-yorks -lawmakers-agree-on-campus-sexual-assault-laws.html?partner=bloomberg. Accessed March 23, 2016.

21. TeensHealth.org, "Date Rape."

22. Anonymous, personal narrative, received November 30, 2015.

a. Valerie Jarrett, "Four Critical Questions for the College Search," October 9, 2015, www .notalone.gov/assets/4-questions-you-should-ask.pdf. Accessed January 2, 2016.

b. Charles M. Blow, "Did *Rolling Stone* Hurt the Quest for Justice?" *New York Times*, April 7, 2015, www.nytimes.com/2015/04/07/opinion/charles-blow-did-rolling-stone-hurt-the -quest-for-justice.html?partner=bloomberg. Accessed March 24, 2016.

c. Kimberly A. Lonsway, Joanne Archambault, and David Lisak, "False Reports: Moving beyond the Issue to Successfully Investigate and Prosecute Non-Stranger Sexual Assault," *Voice*, ndaa.org/pdf/the_voice_vol_3_no_1_2009.pdf. Accessed January 6, 2015.

d. Kathleen Sebelius, "Announcing the Winners of Apps against Abuse Technology Training," *White House Blog*, November 1, 2011, www.whitehouse.gov/blog/2011/11/01/announcing -winners-apps-against-abuse-technology-challenge. Accessed January 6, 2016.

e. Sebelius, "Announcing the Winners."

f. Juana Summers, "Smartphone Apps Help to Battle Campus Sexual Assaults," NPR, August 13, 2014, www.npr.org/2014/08/13/339888170/smartphoneapps-help-to-battle-campus -sexual-assaults. Accessed January 6, 2016.

g. Arvin Donguines, "'The Good Wife' Season 6 News, Spoilers: Finale Episode to Air Nov. 23, Upcoming Episode Indicates Alicia Taking Up College Rape Case," *Christian Post*, www.christianpost.com/news/the-good-wife-season-6-news-spoilers-finale-episode-to-air -nov-23-upcoming-episode-indicates-alicia-taking-up-college-rape-case-129357/. Accessed December 29, 2015.

h. Ariel Kaminer, "New Factor in Campus Sexual Assault Cases: Counsel for the Accused," *New York Times*, November 19, 2014, A22.

i.   Kaminer, "New Factor in Campus Sexual Assault Cases," A22.

j.   Families Advocating for Campus Equality, "About Us" www.facecampusequality.org/about .html. Accessed March 23, 2016.

k.   Tyler Kingkade, "JMU Sued for Punishing Sexual Assault with 'Expulsion after Graduation,'" *Huffington Post*, March 9, 2015, www.huffingtonpost.com/2015/03/09/jmu-sued -sexual-assault_n_6820026.html. Accessed January 6, 2016.

l.   Gary Crowdus, "Transforming Trauma into Political Activism," *Cineaste*, Summer 2015, 44–49.

m.   Kirby Dick and Amy Ziering, "An Open Letter to Florida State University President Thrasher," *Huffington Post*, November 21, 2015, www.huffingtonpost.com/kirby-dick/an- open-letter-to-florida_b_8618724.html. Accessed January 7, 2016. Reprinted with permission.

n.   Amy Ziering, interview questionnaire, received February 9, 2016.

o.   Josh Duboff, "Watch Lady Gaga's Powerful Oscar 2016 Performance," *Vanity Fair*, www. vanityfair.com/hollywood/2016/02/lady-gaga-oscars-performance. Accessed March 23, 2016.

Chapter 3

1.   Alexandra, personal narrative, received November 15, 2015.

2.   Eric Young, "Preliminary Results in Landmark National Survey on Teen Dating Violence Finds Disturbingly High Rates of Victimization and Perpetration by Both Girls and Boys," NORC at the University of Chicago, November 23, 2014, www.norc.org/NewsEvents Publications/PressReleases/Pages/preliminary-results-in-landmark-national-survey-on -teen-dating-violence-finds-disturbingly-high-rates-of-victimization.aspx. Accessed November 27, 2014.

3.   Susan M. Jackson, Fiona Cram, and Fred W. Seymour, "Violence and Sexual Coercion in High School Students' Dating Relationships," *Journal of Family Violence* 15, no. 1 (2000): 23–36.

4.   Love Is Respect, "LGBTQ Abusive Relationships," www.loveisrespect.org/is-this-abuse/ lgbtq-abusive-relationships. Accessed November 8, 2014.

5.   Jackson, Cram, and Seymour, "Violence and Sexual Coercion in High School Students' Dating Relationships," 23–36.

6.   Melinda, personal narrative, received February 9, 2015.

7.   Myra J. Hird and Sue Jackson, "Where 'Angels' and 'Wusses' Fear to Tread: Sexual Coercion in Adolescent Dating Relationships," *Journal of Sociology* 37, no. 1 (2001): 27–43.

8.   Jessica L. Lucero, Arlene N. Weisz, Joanne Smith-Darden, and Steven M. Lucero, "Exploring Gender Differences: Socially Interactive Technology Use/Abuse among Dating Teens," *Journal of Women and Social Work* 29, no. 4 (2014): 478–491.

9.   Janine M. Zweig, Meredith Dank, Jennifer Yahner, and Pamela Lachman, "The Rate of Cyber Abuse among Teens and How It Relates to Other Forms of Teen Dating Violence," *Youth Adolescence* 42, no. 7 (2013): 1063–1077.

10. Janine M. Zweig, Pamela Lachman, Jennifer Yahner, and Meredith Dank, "Correlates of Cyber Dating Abuse among Teens." *Journal of Youth and Adolescence* 43, no. 8 (2013): 1306–1321.

11. Ernest N. Jouriles, David Rosenfield, Renee McDonald, Anne L. Kleinsasser, and M. Catherine Dodson, "Explicit Beliefs about Aggression, Implicit Knowledge Structures, and Teen Dating Violence," *Journal of Abnormal Child Psychology* 41, no. 5 (2013): 789–799.

12. Lindsay, personal narrative, received November 13, 2015.
13. Monika, personal narrative, received February 15, 2015.
14. Deinera Exner-Cortens, John Eckenrode, and Emily Rothman, "Longitudinal Associations between Teen Dating Violence Victimization and Adverse Health Outcomes," *Pediatrics: Official Journal of the American Academy of Pediatrics* 131, no. 1 (2012): 71–78.
15. Zweig et al., "Correlates of Cyber Dating Abuse Among Teens," 1306–1321.

---

a. Chris Lynch, *Inexcusable* (New York: Atheneum Books for Young Readers, 2007).
b. Janine M. Zweig, Pamela Lachman, Jennifer Yahner, and Meredith Dank, "Correlates of Cyber Dating Abuse among Teens," *Journal of Youth and Adolescence* 43, no. 8 (2013): 1306–1321.
c. Project Implicit, implicit.harvard.edu/implicit. Accessed November 19, 2014.
d. Stephenie Meyer, *Twilight* (New York: Little, Brown, 2005).
e. Stephenie Meyer, *Eclipse* (New York: Little, Brown, 2007).
f. Stephenie Meyer, *Breaking Dawn* (New York: Little, Brown, 2008).
g. Victoria E. Collins and Dianne C. Carmody, "Deadly Love: Images of Dating Violence in the 'Twilight Saga,'" *Affilia* 26, no. 4 (2011): 382–394.
h. Swati Avasthi, *Split* (New York: Alfred A. Knopf, 2010).

Chapter 4

1. National Sexual Violence Resource Center, "What Is Child Sexual Abuse?" www.nsvrc.org/sites/default/files/publications_nsvrc_media-packet_1.pdf. Accessed August 11, 2015.
2. Rape, Abuse and Incest National Network, "Incest," www.rainn.org/get-information/types-of-sexual-assault/incest. Accessed March 13, 2015.
3. Spiegel Online International, "The Amstetten Horror: Josef Fritzl Raped Daughter in Front of Children," www.spiegel.de/international/europe/the-amstetten-horror-josef-fritzl-raped-daughter-in-front-of-children-a-551246. Accessed January 9, 2016.
4. Michael Salter, "Grace's Story: Prolonged Incestuous Abuse from Childhood into Adulthood," *Violence Against Women* 19, no. 2 (February 2013): 146–165.
5. Anonymous, personal narrative, received March 9, 2015.
6. Jane Kilby, "Judith Butler, Incest, and the Question of the Child's Love," *Feminist Theory* 11, no. 3 (December 2010): 255–265.
7. Sandra S. Stroebel, Stephen L. O'Keefe, Keith W. Beard, Shih-Ya Kuo, Samuel V. S. Swindell, and Martin J. Kommor, "Father-Daughter Incest: Data from an Anonymous Computerized Survey," *Journal of Child Sexual Abuse* 21, no. 1 (April 2011): 176–199.
8. Stroebel et al., "Father-Daughter Incest," 176–199.
9. Stroebel et al., "Father-Daughter Incest," 176–199.
10. Christine M. DeMaio, Joanne L. Davis, and Daniel W. Smith, "The Use of Clarification Sessions in the Treatment of Incest Victims and Their Families: An Exploratory Study," *Sexual Abuse: A Journal of Research and Treatment* 18, no. 1 (January 2006): 27–39.
11. Peter, personal narrative, received January 9, 2016.
12. Amy Meyers, "A Call to Child Welfare: Protect Children from Sibling Abuse," *Qualitative Social Work* 13, no. 5 (2014): 654–670.
13. Mary J. Phillips-Green, "Sibling Incest," *Family Journal* 10, no. 2 (April 2002): 195–202.

14. Mandy Morrill and Curt Bachman, "Confronting the Gender Myth: An Exploration of Variance in Male versus Female Experience with Sibling Abuse," *Journal of Interpersonal Violence* 28, no. 8 (May 2013): 1693–1708.

15. Karen Griffee, Sam Swindell, Stephen L. O'Keefe, Sandra S. Stroebel, Keith W. Beard, Shih-Ya Kuo, and Walter Stroupe, "Etiological Risk Factors for Sibling Incest: Data from an Anonymous Computer-Assisted Self-Interview," *Sexual Abuse: A Journal of Research and Treatment*, November 27, 2014, www.ncbi.nlm.nih.gov/pubmed/25432976. Accessed November 28, 2015.

16. Sharon Brennan, "Sibling Incest within Violent Families: Children under 12 Seek Nurture," *Health Sociology Review* 15, no. 3 (August 2006): 287–292.

17. Bonnie E. Carlson, Katherine Maciol, and Joanne Schneider, "Sibling Incest: Reports from Forty-One Survivors," *Journal of Child Sexual Abuse* 15, no. 4 (2006): 19–34.

18. Danny, personal narrative, received December 27, 2015.

19. Kristin A. Danni and Gary D. Hampe, "An Analysis of Predictors of Child Sex Offender Types Using Presentence Investigation Reports," *International Journal of Offender Therapy and Comparative Criminology* 44, no. 4 (August 2000): 490–504.

20. National Sexual Violence Resource Center, "Statistics about Sexual Violence," www.nsvrc.org/sites/default/files/publications_nsvrc_media-packet_1.pdf. Accessed August 11, 2015.

21. Beth Holger-Ambrose, Cheree Langmade, Laurel D. Edinburgh, and Elizabeth Saewyc, "The Illusions and Juxtapositions of Commercial Sexual Exploitation among Youth: Identifying Effective Street-Outreach Strategies," *Journal of Child Sexual Abuse* 22, no. 1 (2013): 326–340.

22. Holger-Ambrose et al., "The Illusions and Juxtapositions of Commercial Sexual Exploitation among Youth," 326–340.

23. Darkness to Light, "Child Abuse Statistics," www.d2l.org/site/c.4dICIJOkGcISE/b.6143427/k.38C5/Child_Sexual_Abuse_Statistics. Accessed August 12, 2015.

24. US Department of Justice, "A Parent's Guide to Internet Safety," www.fbi.gov/stats-services/publications/parent-guide. Accessed August 12, 2015.

25. Darkness to Light, "Child Abuse Statistics."

26. Kathy, personal narrative, postmarked January 23, 2016.

27. Carolyn Copps Hartley, "Incest Offenders' Perceptions of Their Motives to Sexually Offend within Their Past and Current Life Context," *Journal of Interpersonal Violence* 16, no. 5 (May 2001): 459–475.

28. National Sexual Violence Resource Center, "What Is Child Sexual Abuse?"

29. National Sexual Violence Resource Center, "What Is Child Sexual Abuse?"

30. Jannina, personal narrative, received July 23, 2015.

---

a. John E. B. Myers, "A Short History of Child Protection in America," *Family Law Quarterly* 42, no. 3 (Fall 2008): 449–463.

b. Laura Wiess, *Such a Pretty Girl* (New York: MTV Books, Simon and Schuster, 2007).

c. *In a Town This Size*, directed by Patrick Viersen Brown (First Run Features, 2011), www.inatownthissize.com. Accessed January 10, 2016.

d. Ellen Hopkins, *Identical* (New York: Margaret K. McElderry Books, Simon and Schuster, 2010).

e. David Collins, "Suit: Connecticut Scoutmaster Abused 19 Kids in '60s, '70s," *Big Story*, November 17, 2015, www.bigstory.ap.org/article/541b85115a6346caa2436a46b1caa833/suit-connecticut-scoutmaster-abused-19-kids-60s-70s. Accessed January 10, 2016.

Chapter 5

1. Samantha Gluck, "Effects of Rape: Psychological and Physical Effects of Rape," Healthy Place, www.healthyplace.com/abuse/rape/effects-of-rape-psychological-and-physical-effects-of-rape. Accessed August 15, 2015.
2. Starre Vartan, "The Lifelong Consequences of Rape," *Pacific Standard*, www.psmag.com/health-and-behavior/lifelong-consequences-rape-96056. Accessed August 15, 2015.
3. Rape, Abuse and Incest National Network, "Sexually Transmitted Infections-STIs and STDs," www.rainn.org/get-information/effects-of-sexual-assault/sexually-transmitted-infections. Accessed November 19, 2015.
4. American Psychiatric Association, *Diagnostic and Statistical Manual of Mental Disorders* (Washington, DC: American Psychiatric Publishing, 2013), 208–211.
5. Matthew T. Tull and Lizabeth Roemer, "Alternative Explanations of Emotional Numbing of Posttraumatic Stress Disorder: An Examination of Hyperarousal and Experiential Avoidance." *Journal of Psychopathology & Behavioral Assessment* 25, no. 3 (September 2003): 147–154.
6. Christina Enevoldsen, "Dealing with Triggers of Abuse," Overcoming Sexual Abuse, January 23, 2012, www.overcomingsexualabuse.com/2012/01/23/dealing-with-triggers-of-abuse. Accessed January 10, 2016.
7. National Institute of Mental Health, "Post-Traumatic Stress Disorder (PTSD)," www.nimh.nih.gov/health/topics/post-traumatic-stress-disorder-ptsd/index.shtml#part3. Accessed August 15, 2015.
8. American Psychiatric Association, *Diagnostic and Statistical Manual of Mental Disorders*, 271–272.
9. American Psychiatric Association, *Diagnostic and Statistical Manual of Mental Disorders*, 271–272.
10. Toby, personal narrative, received November 25, 2015.
11. National Institute of Mental Health, "Post-Traumatic Stress Disorder (PTSD)."
12. Vartan, "The Lifelong Consequences of Rape."
13. Rape, Abuse and Incest National Network, "Self-Harm," www.rainn.org/get-information/effects-of-sexual-assault/self-harm. Accessed August 15, 2015.
14. Rape, Abuse and Incest National Network, "Flashbacks," www.rainn.org/effects-of-sexual-assault/flashbacks. Accessed August 15, 2015.
15. American Psychiatric Association, *Diagnostic and Statistical Manual of Mental Disorders*, 160–161.
16. Rape, Abuse and Incest National Network, "Depression," www.rainn.org/get-information/effects-of-sexual-assault/depression. Accessed August 15, 2015.
17. Rape, Abuse and Incest National Network, "Substance Abuse," www.rainn.org/get-information/effects-of-sexual-assault/substance-abuse. Accessed August 15, 2015.
18. Rape, Abuse and Incest National Network, "Dissociation," www.rainn.org/get-information/effects-of-sexual-assault/dissociation. Accessed August 15, 2015.
19. Nicole P. Yuan, Mary P. Koss, and Mirto Stone, "The Psychological Consequences of Sexual Trauma," National Online Resource Center on Violence Against Women, www.vawnet.org/applied-research-papers. Accessed August 15, 2015.
20. Rape, Abuse and Incest National Network, "Dissociation."
21. Jannina, personal narrative, received July 23, 2015.

22. Rape, Abuse and Incest National Network, "Eating Disorders," www.rainn.org/get -information/effects-of-sexual-assault/eating-disorders. Accessed August 15, 2015.

23. Rape, Abuse and Incest National Network, "Sleep Disorders," www.rainn.org/get -information/effects-of-sexual-assault/sleep-disorders. Accessed August 15, 2015.

a. Taysa, personal narrative, received December 3, 2015.

b. Lindsey Tanner, "Many Teen Sex Assault Victims Get Subpar ER Care, Study Says," *Big Story*, November 2, 2015, www.bigstory.ap.org/article/1debcf0b40fb4d67b45aa9bd07e3 e9d6/many-teen-sex-assault-victims-get-subpar-er-care-study-says. Accessed March 27, 2016.

c. Kate Manne, "Why I Use Trigger Warnings," *New York Times*, September 19, 2015, www .nytimes.com/2015/09/20/opinion/sunday/why-i-use-trigger-warnings.html?_r=0. Accessed January 11, 2016.

d. Greg Lukianoff and Jonathan Haidt, "The Coddling of the American Mind," *Atlantic*, September 2015, 42–52.

e. Meagan, personal narrative, received December 10, 2015.

f. Elizabeth Fuller, "For Sexual Crime Victims, TSA Pat-Downs Can Be 'Re-traumatizing,'" *Christian Science Monitor*, November 24, 2010, 7.

g. Anonymous, personal narrative, received December 4, 2015.

h. Marissa, personal narrative, received September 30, 2015.

i. Destiny, personal narrative, received November 11, 2015.

Chapter 6

1. Hayley, personal narrative, received December 3, 2015.
2. Sarah E. Ullman, *Talking about Sexual Assault: Society's Response to Survivors* (Washington, DC: American Psychological Association, 2010), 36.
3. Ullman, *Talking about Sexual Assault*, 50–51.
4. Toby, personal narrative, received November 25, 2015.
5. Ullman, *Talking about Sexual Assault*, 47.
6. Ullman, *Talking about Sexual Assault*, 47–48.
7. Ullman, *Talking about Sexual Assault*, 49–50.
8. Ullman, *Talking about Sexual Assault*, 50.
9. Rape, Abuse and Incest National Network, "Reporting to Law Enforcement," www.rainn .org/get-information/legal-information/reporting-rape. Accessed August 20, 2015.
10. Sarah E. Ullman, "Correlates and Consequences of Adult Sexual Assault Disclosure," *Journal of Interpersonal Violence* 11, no. 4 (December 1996): 554–571.
11. Rape, Abuse and Incest National Network, "What Is a Rape Kit?" www.rainn.org/get -information/sexual-assault-recovery/rape-kit. Accessed January 16, 2016.
12. Rape, Abuse and Incest National Network, "What Is a Rape Kit?"
13. Rape, Abuse and Incest National Network, "What Is a Rape Kit?"
14. Ullman, *Talking about Sexual Assault*, 93.
15. Rape, Abuse and Incest National Network, "Reporting to Law Enforcement."
16. Rape, Abuse and Incest National Network, "What Is a Rape Kit?"

17. Rape, Abuse and Incest National Network, "Communicating with Law Enforcement," www .rainn.org/get-info/legal-information/communicating-with-law-enforcement. Accessed August 21, 2015.

18. Lindsay M. Orchowski and Christine A. Gidycz, "To Whom Do College Women Confide Following Sexual Assault? A Prospective Study of Predictors of Sexual Assault Disclosure and Social Reactions," *Violence Against Women* 18, no. 3 (2012): 264–288.

19. Ullman, *Talking about Sexual Assault*, 95.

20. Ullman, *Talking about Sexual Assault*, 95–99.

21. Meagan, personal narrative, received December 10, 2015.

22. Ullman, *Talking about Sexual Assault*, 62.

23. Rape, Abuse and Incest National Network, "How to Respond to a Survivor," www.rainn.org/ get-information/sexual-assault-recovery/respond-to-a-survivor. Accessed August 21, 2015.

24. Ullman, *Talking about Sexual Assault*, 63.

25. Jannina, personal narrative, received July 23, 2015.

26. Ullman, *Talking about Sexual Assault*, 65.

27. Orchowski and Gidycz, "To Whom Do College Women Confide Following Sexual Assault?" 264–288.

28. Lindsay M. Orchowski and Christine A. Gidycz, "Psychological Consequences Associated with Positive and Negative Responses to Disclosure of Sexual Assault among College Women: A Prospective Study," *Violence Against Women* 21, no. 7 (2015): 803–823.

29. Ullman, *Talking about Sexual Assault*, 69.

30. Ullman, *Talking about Sexual Assault*, 67.

31. Ullman, *Talking about Sexual Assault*, 68.

32. Taysa, personal narrative, received December 3, 2015.

33. Rebecca Campbell, Megan R. Greeson, Giannina Fehler-Cabral, and Angie C. Kennedy, "Pathways to Help: Adolescent Sexual Assault Victims' Disclosure and Help-Seeking Experiences," *Violence Against Women* 21, no. 7 (2015): 824–847.

34. Kelli, personal narrative, received October 10, 2015.

a. "Lights Out," *Glee*, season 4, episode 12, Fox Network, April 25, 2013.

b. *Outlawed in Pakistan*, directed by Habiba Nosheen and Hilke Schellmann (PBS, 2013), www .pbs.org/wgbh/frontline/film/outlawed-in-pakistan/. Accessed January 16, 2016.

c. Rachele Alpine, *Canary* (New York: Medallion Press, 2013).

d. "Maya Angelou: From Child Rape Victim to Medal of Honor Winner," *Newsmax*, May 28, 2014, www.newsmax.com/Newsfront/Angelou-obit-freedom-poet/2014/05/28/id/573894/. Accessed January 16, 2016.

e. Chris Heath, "Fiona: The Caged Bird Sings," *Rolling Stone*, January 22, 1998, www.rolling stone.com/music/news/fiona-the-caged-bird-sings-19980122. Accessed January 16, 2016.

f. "Oprah Talks to Fantasia," *O Magazine*, www.oprah.com/omagazine/Oprah-Talks-to-Fantasia-Barrino. Accessed January 17, 2016.

g. Rachel Levy, "'I Said I Wasn't Going to Cry': Teri Hatcher Breaks Down in Tears after Giving Emotional Speech about Sexual Abuse at United Nations," *Daily Mail*, November 25, 2014, www.dailymail.co.uk/tvshowbiz/article-2849423/Teri-Hatcher-breaks-tears-giving -emotional-speech-sexal-abuse-United-Nations. Accessed January 17, 2016.

h. Chelsea White, "'I Am a Survivor of Rape, Sexual Assault and Incest': Actress Ashley Judd Bravely Tells of Teenage Abuse as She Hits Back at Twitter Trolls," *Daily Mail*, March 19, 2015, www.dailymail.co.uk/tvshowbiz/article-3003367/Ashley-Judd-recalls-personal-history

-rape-incest-powerful-essay-addressing-offline-gender-violence-Twitter-abuse-college
-basketball-game. Accessed January 17, 2016.

i. Andrea Mandell, "Lady Gaga Expands on Rape at Nineteen," *USA Today*, December 11, 2015, www.usatoday.com/story/life/people/2015/12/11/lady-gaga-opens-up-about-rape -at-19/77155060/. Accessed January 17, 2016.

j. "Lady Gaga—Til It Happens to You (at the Oscars 2016)," YouTube video, filmed February 2016, www.youtube.com/watch?v=QEjaXXu69Us. Accessed March 27, 2016.

k. Elizabeth Fry, "A Childhood Biography of Oprah Winfrey," *About Entertainment*, www .oprah.about.com/od/oprahbiography/p/oprahchildhood. Accessed January 17, 2016.

l. Oprah.com, "Tyler Perry's Traumatic Childhood," www.oprah.com/oprahshow/Tyler -Perry-Speaks-Out-About-Being-Molested-and-the-Aftermath. Accessed January 17, 2016.

m. Sadie Whitelocks, "'Being a Victim Makes You Lazy': Gabrielle Union on How She Overcame Being Raped at Gunpoint Aged Nineteen," *Daily Mail*, February 24, 2014, www.dailymail .co.uk/femail/article-2566825/Being-victim-makes-lazy-Gabrielle-Union-overcame-raped -gunpoint-aged-19. Accessed January 17, 2016.

n. Samantha Chang, "Queen Latifah Talks Weight and Alcoholism: I Was Molested as a Child," *Examiner*, December 11, 2013, www.examiner.com/article/queen-latifah-talks-body-image -and-alcoholism-i-love-my-curves. Accessed January 17, 2016.

Chapter 7

1. Kathryn M. Ryan, "The Relationship between Rape Myths and Sexual Scripts: The Social Construction of Rape," *Sex Roles* 65, nos. 11–12 (December 2011): 774–782.
2. Jericho M. Hockett, Donald A. Saucier, and Caitlyn Badke, "Rape Myths, Rape Scripts, and Common Rape Experiences of College Women: Differences in Perceptions of Women Who Have Been Raped," *Violence Against Women* 21, no. 8 (August 13, 2015): 1–17.
3. Ryan, "The Relationship between Rape Myths and Sexual Scripts," 774–782
4. Ryan, "The Relationship between Rape Myths and Sexual Scripts," 774–782.
5. Ryan, "The Relationship between Rape Myths and Sexual Scripts," 774–782.
6. Sarah E. Ullman, *Talking about Sexual Assault: Society's Response to Survivors* (Washington, DC: American Psychological Association, 2010), 15–16.
7. Arnold S. Kahn and Virginia Andreoli Mathie, "Rape Scripts and Rape Acknowledgment," *Psychology of Women Quarterly* 18, no. 1 (March 1994): 53–66.
8. Katherine A. Black and Kathy A. McCloskey, "Predicting Date Rape Perceptions: The Effects of Gender, Gender Role Attitudes, and Victim Resistance," *Violence Against Women* 19, no. 8 (2013): 949–967.
9. Rape, Abuse and Incest National Network, "Who Are the Victims?" www.rainn.org/get -information/statistics/sexual-assault-victims. Accessed March 28, 2016.
10. Rebecca M. Hayes, Katherine Lorenz, and Kristin A. Bell, "Victim Blaming Others: Rape Myth Acceptance and the Just World Belief," *Feminist Criminology* 8, no. 3 (2013): 202–220.
11 Black and McCloskey, "Predicting Date Rape Perceptions," 949–967.
12. Avigail More, "She Dresses to Attract, He Perceives Seduction: A Gender Gap in Attribution of Intent to Women's Revealing Style of Dress and Its Relation in Blaming the Victims of Sexual Violence," *Journal of International Women's Studies* 11, no. 4 (May 2010): 115–127.
13. More, "She Dresses to Attract, He Perceives Seduction," 115–127.
14. Hockett et al., "Rape Myths, Rape Scripts," 1–17.

15. Hockett et al., "Rape Myths, Rape Scripts," 1–17.

16. Rape, Assault and Incest National Network, "Statistics," www.rainn.org/statistics. Accessed August 26, 2015.

17. Rebecca L. Vonderhaar and Dianne Cyr Carmody, "There Are No 'Innocent Victims': The Influence of Just World Beliefs and Prior Victimization on Rape Myth Acceptance," *Journal of Interpersonal Violence* 30, no. 10 (2015): 1615–1632.

18. GRACE, "Final Report: For the Investigative Review of Sexual Abuse Disclosures and Institutional Responses at Bob Jones University," static1.squarespace.com/static/54596334 e4b0780b44555981/t/552e9be7e4b0498e9c4b8c24/1429117927390/Bob+Jones+U+Final +Report.pdf. Accessed January 21, 2016.

19. GRACE, "Final Report."

20. Claire Gordon, "Rape Victims 'Hopeless' after Bob Jones University Response," *Aljazeera America*, america.aljazeera.com/watch/shows/america-tonight/articles/2015/3/30/bob-jones -university-sexual-abuse.html. Accessed January 21, 2016.

21. Tiffany, personal narrative, received July 30, 2015.

22. Katie Edwards, Jessica A. Turchik, Christina M. Dardis, Nicole Reynolds, and Christine A. Gidycz, "Rape Myths: History, Individual and Institutional-Level Presence, and Implications for Change," *Sex Roles* 65, nos. 11–12 (December 2011): 761–773.

23. Edwards et al., "Rape Myths," 761–773.

24. Daniele E. Doty, "A System Appallingly Out of Balance: *Morgan v. State* and the Rights of Defendants and Victims in Sexual Assault Prosecutions," *Alaska Law Review* 32, no. 2 (December 2015): 249–272.

25. Peter A. Newcombe, Julie van den Eynde, Diane Hafner, and Lesley Jolly, "Attributions of Responsibility for Rape: Differences across Familiarity of Situation, Gender, and Acceptance of Rape Myths." *Journal of Applied Social Psychology* 38, no. 7 (July 2008): 1736–1754.

26. Melanie S. Harned, "Understanding Women's Labeling of Unwanted Sexual Experiences with Dating Partners," *Violence Against Women* 11, no. 3 (March 2005): 374–413.

27. Sandra L. Schneider and Robert C. Wright. "Understanding Denial in Sexual Offenders," *Trauma, Violence and Abuse* 5, no. 1 (January 2004): 3–20.

28. Naomi Schaefer Riley, "College Women Don't Get Wasted on Campus," *USA Today*, May 10, 2011, A9.

29. Wilma King, "Prematurely Knowing of Evil Things: The Sexual Abuse of African American Girls and Young Women in Slavery and Freedom," *Journal of African American History* 99, no. 3 (Summer 2014): 173–196.

30. Women of Color Network, "Sexual Violence Facts," www.doj.state.or.us/victims/pdf/ women_of_color_network_facts_sexual_violence_2006.pdf. Accessed December 26, 2015.

31. Victoria Ybanez, "Domestic Violence: An Introduction to the Social and Legal Issues for Native Women," chapter 3 in *Sharing Our Stories of Survival*, ed. Sarah Deer et al. (New York: Altamira Press, 2008), 50.

32. Women of Color Network, "Sexual Violence Facts."

33. Jessica Lussenhop, "Daniel Holtzclaw Trial: Standing with 'Imperfect' Accusers," *BBC News Magazine*, November 13, 2015, www.bbc.com/news/magazine-34791191. Accessed January 24, 2016.

34. Elliot Hannon, "Oklahoma Cop Convicted of Rape, Sexual Assault On-Duty Sentenced to 263 Years in Jail," *Slate*, www.slate.com/blogs/the_slatest/2016/01/21/oklahoma_cop_daniel_ holtzclaw_gets_life_in_jail_for_sexual_assaults_on_duty.html. Accessed January 24, 2016.

35. Megan A. Alderdenl and Sarah E. Ullman, "Creating a More Complete and Current Picture: Examining Police and Prosecutor Decision-Making When Processing Sexual Assault Cases," *Violence Against Women* 18, no. 5 (2012): 525–551.

36. Anna Stolley Persky, "Prosecutors Battle the Wall of Silence around Sex Assault in Religious Communities," *ABA Journal* 99, no. 12 (December 2013): 46–51.

37. Alana Prochuk, "Rape Culture Is Real, and Yes, We've Had Enough," *Women Against Violence Against Women*, www.wavaw.ca/rape-culture-is-real-and-yes-weve-had-enough. Accessed January 25, 2016.

38. Rebecca M. Hayes, Katherine Lorenz, and Kristin A. Bell, "Victim Blaming Others: Rape Myth Acceptance and the Just World Belief," *Feminist Criminology* 8, no. 3 (2013): 202–222.

39. Ryan, "The Relationship between Rape Myths and Sexual Scripts," 774–782.

40. Laura Bates, "Does Facebook Have a Problem with Women?" *Guardian*, February 19, 2013, www.theguardian.com/lifeandstyle/2013/feb/19/facebook-images-rape-domestic-violence. Accessed January 25, 2016.

41. Prochuk, "Rape Culture Is Real."

42. "No Comment," *Ms. Magazine*, Spring 2005, msmagazine.com/nocommentarchive.asp. Accessed January 25, 2016.

43. Laura Stampler, "SlutWalks Sweep the Nation," *Huffington Post*, June 20, 2011, www.huffingtonpost.com/2011/04/20/slutwalk-united-states-city_n_851725.html. Accessed January 25, 2016.

---

a. Courtney Summers, *Some Girls Are* (New York: St. Martin's Griffin, 2010).

b. Ashley, personal narrative, received November 24, 2015.

c. Alina Klein, *Rape Girl* (South Hampton, NH: Namelos, 2012).

d. Avril Lavigne, "Smile" in *Goodbye Lullaby*, RCA Records (2011).

e. Stephanie Marcus, "Maroon 5's 'Animals' Video Slammed by Sexual Assault Support Group," *Huffington Post*, October 2, 2014, www.huffingtonpost.com/2014/10/02/maroon-5-animals-slammed_n_5920340.html. Accessed January 25, 2016.

f. Robin Thicke, T. I., and Pharrell Williams, "Blurred Lines," in *Blurred Lines*, Star Trak Recordings (2013).

g. Carrie Underwood, "Before He Cheats," in *Some Hearts*, Arista Nashville (2005).

h. Marya Hannun, "'Baby It's Cold Outside' Was Once an Anthem for Progressive Women. What Happened?" *Washington Post*, December 19, 2014, www.washingtonpost.com/posteverything/wp/2014/12/19/baby-its-cold-outside-was-once-an-anthem-for-progressive-women-what-happened/. Accessed January 25, 2016.

Chapter 8

1. Jacqueline M. Golding, Sharon C. Wilsnack, and M. Lynne Cooper, "Sexual Assault History and Social Support: Six General Population Studies," *Journal of Traumatic Stress* 15, no. 3 (June 2002): 187–197.

2. Susan E. Borja, Jennifer L. Callahan, and Patricia J. Long, "Positive and Negative Adjustment and Social Support of Sexual Assault Survivors," *Journal of Traumatic Stress* 19, no. 6 (December 2006): 905–914.

3. Gillian E. Mason, Sarah Ullman, Susan E. Long, LaDonna Long, and Laura Starzynski, "Social Support and Risk of Sexual Assault Revictimization," *Journal of Community Psychology* 37, no. 1 (2009): 58–72.
4. Mason et al., "Social Support," 58–72.
5. Deborah, personal narrative, received February 2, 2015.
6. Jeffrey L. Todahl, Deanna Linville, Amy Bustin, and Jeff M. Gau, "Sexual Assault Support Services and Community Systems: Understanding the Critical Issues and Needs in the LGBTQ Community," *Violence Against Women* 15, no. 8 (August 2009): 952–976.
7. Women of Color Network, "Sexual Violence Facts," www.doj.state.or.us/victims/pdf/women_of_color_network_facts_sexual_violence_2006.pdf. Accessed December 26, 2015.
8. Rape, Abuse and Incest National Network, "Find Help Near You," centers.rainn.org. Accessed October 7, 2015.
9. Toby, personal narrative, received November 25, 2015.
10. Destiny, personal narrative, received November 11, 2015.

a. Sexual Assault Awareness Month, "SAAM History," www.nsvrc.org/saam/about/history. Accessed January 29, 2016.
b. Daisy Whitney, *The Mockingbirds* (New York: Little, Brown Books for Young Readers, 2012).
c. *The Invisible War*, directed by Kirby Dick (PBS, 2012), www.pbs.org/independentlens/films/invisible-war. Accessed January 29, 2016.

Chapter 9

1. Sheryle Vilenica, Jane Shakespeare-Finch, and Patricia Obst, "Exploring the Process of Meaning Making in Healing and Growth after Childhood Sexual Assault: A Case Study Approach," *Counseling Psychology Quarterly* 26, no. 1 (March 2012): 39–54.
2. Vilenica et al., "Exploring the Process of Meaning Making," 39–54.
3. Mary P. Koss and Aurelio Jose Figueredo, "Change in Cognitive Mediators of Rape's Impact on Psychosocial Health across 2 Years of Recovery," *Journal of Consulting and Clinical Psychology* 72, no. 6 (2004): 1063–1072.
4. Thanomjit Phanichrat and Julia M. Townshend, "Coping Strategies Used by Survivors of Childhood Sexual Abuse on the Journey to Recovery," *Journal of Child Sexual Abuse* 19, no. 1 (2010): 62–78.
5. Vilenica et al., "Exploring the Process of Meaning Making," 39–54.
6. Vilenica et al., "Exploring the Process of Meaning Making," 39–54.
7. Claudia, phone interview, conducted February 20, 2015.
8. Vilenica et al., "Exploring the Process of Meaning Making," 39–54.
9. Phanichrat and Townshend, "Coping Strategies Used by Survivors," 62–78.
10. Meagan, personal narrative, received December 10, 2015.
11. Vilenica et al., "Exploring the Process of Meaning Making," 39–54.
12. Vilenica et al., "Exploring the Process of Meaning Making," 39–54.
13. Laurie, phone interview, conducted July 28, 2015.
14. Natasha Tracy, "Rape Therapy: A Treatment for Rape Victims," *Healthy Place*, www.healthyplace.com/abuse/rape/rape-therapy-a-treatment-for-rape-victims. Accessed August 15, 2015.
15. Tracy, "Rape Therapy."

16. Tracy, "Rape Therapy."
17. Edna B. Foa, Terence M. Keane, Matthew J. Friedman, and Judith A. Cohen, *Effective Treatments for PTSD* (New York: Guilford Press, 2009), 144.
18. Patricia A. Resick, Pallavi Nishith, Terri L. Weaver, Millie C. Astin, and Catherine A. Feuer, "A Comparison of Cognitive-Processing Therapy with Prolonged Exposure and a Waiting Condition for the Treatment of Chronic Posttraumatic Stress Disorder in Female Rape Victims," *Journal of Consulting and Clinical Psychology* 70, no. 4 (August 2002): 867–879.
19. EMDR International Association, "How Does EMDR Work?" www.emdria.org/?119. Accessed January 30, 2016.
20. Foa et al., *Effective Treatments for PTSD*, 288.
21. Foa et al., *Effective Treatments for PTSD*, 515.
22. Sherry A. Falsetti, Heidi S. Resnick, and Joanne L. Davis, "Multiple Channel Exposure Therapy for Women with PTSD and Comorbid Panic Attacks," *Cognitive Behaviour Therapy* 37, no. 2 (June 2008): 117–130.
23. Anonymous, follow-up questionnaire, received December 3, 2015.
24. Vilenica et al., "Exploring the Process of Meaning Making," 39–54.
25. Kim M. Anderson and Catherine Hiersteiner, "Recovering from Childhood Sexual Abuse: Is a 'Storybook Ending' Possible?" *American Journal of Family Therapy* 36, no. 1 (2008): 413–424.
26. Crystal L. Park and Carol Joyce Blumberg. "Disclosing Trauma through Writing: Testing the Meaning-Making Hypothesis," *Cognitive Therapy & Research* 26, no. 5 (October 2002): 597–616.
27. Alexandra M. Dick, Barbara L. Niles, Amy E. Street, Dawn M. DiMartino, and Karen S. Mitchell, "Examining Mechanisms of Change in a Yoga Intervention for Women: The Influence of Mindfulness, Psychological Flexibility, and Emotion Regulation on PTSD Symptoms," *Journal of Clinical Psychology* 70, no. 12 (December 1, 2014): 1170–1182.
28. Vernon A. Barnes, Andrea Monto, Jennifer J. Williams, and John L. Rigg, "Impact of Transcendental Meditation on Psychotropic Medication Use among Active Duty Military Service Members with Anxiety and PTSD," *Military Medicine* 181, no. 1 (January 1, 2016): 56–63.
29. Robert W. Motta, Meredith E. McWilliams, Jennifer T. Schwartz, and Robert S. Cavera, "The Role of Exercise in Reducing Childhood and Adolescent PTSD, Anxiety, and Depression," *Journal of Applied School Psychology* 28, no. 3 (July–September 2012): 224–238.
30. Phanichrat and Townshend, "Coping Strategies Used by Survivors," 62–78.
31. Mayo Clinic staff, "Post-Traumatic Stress Disorder," Mayo Clinic, www.mayoclinic.org/diseases-conditions/post-traumatic-stress-disorder/basics/treatment/con-20022540. Accessed April 1, 2016.
32. Destiny, personal narrative, received November 11, 2015.
33. Anderson and Hiersteiner, "Recovering from Childhood Sexual Abuse," 413–424.
34. Phanichrat and Townshend, "Coping Strategies Used by Survivors," 62–78.
35. Vilenica et al., "Exploring the Process of Meaning Making," 39–54.
36. Carolyn, personal narrative, received November 3, 2015.

a. Toby, personal narrative, received November 25, 2015.
b. Lynn Hirschberg, "The Audacity of 'Precious.'" *New York Times Magazine*, October 21, 2009, www.nytimes.com/2009/10/25/magazine/25precious-t.html. Accessed January 30, 2016.
c. Colleen Clayton, *What Happens Next* (New York: Poppy, 2013).

Chapter 10

1. Jannina, personal narrative, received July 23, 2015.
2. Tiffany, personal narrative, received July 30, 2015.
3. Maia Szalavitz, "What Bystanders Can Do to Stop Rape," *Time*, January 11, 2013, www.healthland.time.com/2013/01/11/what-bystanders-can-do-to-stop-rape. Accessed November 28, 2015.
4. Laura Starecheski, "The Power of the Peer Group in Preventing Campus Rape," NPR, August 18, 2014, www.npr.org/sections/health-shots/2014/08/18/339593542/the-power-of-the-peer-group-in-preventing-campus=rape. Accessed November 28, 2015.
5. Starecheski, "The Power of the Peer Group."
6. Step Up! "Strategies for Effective Helping," stepupprogram.org/facilitators/strategies-effective-helping/. Accessed November 28, 2015.
7. Step Up! "Strategies for Effective Helping."
8. Becky, personal narrative, received February 20, 2015.
9. Taysa, personal narrative, received December 3, 2015.
10. Jordan Michel Smith, "Dated Rape," *Mother Jones*, January/February 2015, 8–11.
11. Smith, "Dated Rape," 8–11.
12. Kevin Johnson, "FBI Changes Definition of Rape to Add Men as Victims," *USA Today*, January 6, 2012, A1.
13. Smith, "Dated Rape," 8–11.
14. Melanie Eversley, "System Tackles Backlog of Rape Evidence," *USA Today*, June 8, 2015, A5.
15. Natasha's Justice Project, "Statistics," www.natashasjusticeproject.org/about/statistics. Accessed December 22, 2015.
16. Eversley, "System Tackles Backlog of Rape Evidence," A5.
17. Rape, Assault and Incest National Network, "Public Policy," www.rainn.org/public-policy. Accessed December 18, 2015.
18. Laurie, phone interview, July 28, 2015.

a. Jon Krakauer, *Missoula* (New York: Anchor Books, 2016).
b. PACT5, "PACT5 Mission Statement," www.pact5.org. Accessed November 28, 2015.
c. Anita, in-person interview, February 19, 2015.

Resources

Organizations and Websites

Campus Assault

End Rape on Campus: 1-424-777-3762, www.endrapeoncampus.org
Know Your IX: www.knowyourix.org
The National Center for Victims of Crime: www.victimsofcrime.org
National Sexual Assault Hotline: 1-800-656-HOPE
National Sexual Assault Online Hotline: www.online.rainn.org
Students Active for Ending Rape (SAFER): www.safercampus.org

Child Sexual Abuse

Darkness to Light: www.d2l.org
The National Center for Victims of Crime: www.victimsofcrime.org
National Sexual Assault Hotline: 1-800-656-HOPE
National Sexual Assault Online Hotline: www.online.rainn.org

LGBTQ Teens

GLBT National Help Center: www.glnh.org
The Northwest Network: www.nwnetwork.org
The Trevor Project: www.thetrevorproject.org

Mental Health

National Eating Disorder Association: 1-800-931-2237, www.nationaleating
    disorders.org
National Sexual Assault Hotline: 1-800-656-4673 or chat online at www.online
    .rainn.org
National Suicide Prevention Lifeline: 1-800-273-8255
Self-injury Outreach and Support (SiOS): www.sioutreach.org

Substance Abuse and Mental Health Services Administration: www.findtreatment
.samhsa.gov

Substance Abuse Treatment Referral Helpline: 1-800-662-4357

Teen Dating Violence

Break the Cycle: Empowering Youth to End Domestic Violence: www.breakth
ecycle.org

Love Is Respect: www.loveisrespect.org

The National Center for Victims of Crime: www.victimsofcrime.org

The National Domestic Violence Hotline: www.thehotline.org

National Sexual Assault Online Hotline: www.online.rainn.org

No More: Together We Can End Domestic Violence and Sexual Assault: www
.nomore.org

Additional Organizations

1 in 6: www.1in6.org

Break the Cycle: www.breakthecycle.org

INCITE! Women of Color against Violence: www.incite-national.org

The Joyful Heart Foundation: www.joyfulheartfoundation.org

Male Survivor: www.malesurvivor.org

Minnesota Indian Women's Sexual Assault Coalition: www.miwsac.org

National Organization of Asians and Pacific Islanders Ending Sexual Violence:
www.napiesv.org

The National Organization of Sisters of Color Ending Sexual Assault: www
.sisterslead.org

National Sexual Violence Resource Center: www.nsvrc.org

Pandora's Project: www.pandys.org

Rape, Abuse and Incest National Network: www.rainn.org

Safe Horizon: www.safehorizon.org

Survivors Network of Those Abused by Priests: www.snapnetwork.org

Fiction: Novels

Canary by Rachele Alpine (New York: Medallion Press, 2013).

Fault Line by Christa Desir (New York: Simon Pulse, 2013).

Identical by Ellen Hopkins (New York: Margaret K. McElderry Books, Simon
and Schuster, 2010).

The Mockingbirds by Daisy Whitney (New York: Little, Brown Books for Young Readers, 2012).

Rape Girl by Alina Klein (South Hampton: Namelos, 2012).

Some Girls Are by Courtney Summers (New York: St. Martin's Griffin, 2010).

Something Happened by Greg Logsted (New York: Simon Pulse, 2008).

Split by Swati Avasthi (New York: Alfred A. Knopf, 2010).

Such a Pretty Girl by Laura Wiess (New York: MTV Books, Simon and Schuster, 2007).

What Happens Next by Colleen Clayton (New York: Poppy, 2013).

Nonfiction Books

Depression: The Ultimate Teen Guide by Tina Schwartz, It Happened to Me, number 42 (Lanham, MD: Rowman & Littlefield, 2014).

Eating Disorders: The Ultimate Teen Guide by Jessica R. Greene, It Happened to Me, number 39 (Lanham, MD: Rowman & Littlefield, 2014).

Missoula by Jon Krakauer (New York: Anchor Books, 2016).

Self-Injury: The Ultimate Teen Guide by Judy Dodge Cummings, It Happened to Me, number 46 (Lanham, MD: Rowman & Littlefield, 2015).

Substance Abuse: The Ultimate Teen Guide by Sheri Mabry Bestor, It Happened to Me, number 36 (Lanham, MD: Rowman & Littlefield, 2013).

Films

Precious: Based on the Novel Push by Sapphire. DVD. Directed by Lee Daniels (2009; Lionsgate, 2010). Running time: 1 hour, 50 minutes.

Documentaries

Frontline: Outlawed in Pakistan. DVD. Directed by Habiba Nosheen and Hilke Schellmann (2013; PBS, 2013). Running Time: 52 minutes.

The Hunting Ground. DVD. Directed by Kirby Dick (2015; Anchor Bay, 2015). Running time: 1 hour, 43 minutes.

In a Town This Size. DVD. Directed by Patrick Viersen Brown (2011; First Run Features, 2013). Running time: 1 hour, 11 minutes.

The Invisible War. DVD. Directed by Kirby Dick (2012; Documram, 2012). Running time: 1 hour, 39 minutes.

Tapestries of Hope. Directed by Michealene Cristini Risley (2009). Running time: 1 hour, 16 minutes.

Index

About the Author

Olivia Ghafoerkhan teaches college composition at a community college near Washington, DC, where she lives with her husband and four children. She earned her BA from Florida State University, where she majored in English and minored in women's studies, and her MFA from Hamline University. For this book she spent over a year studying sexual assault and speaking with survivors. In addition to interviewing more than forty survivors for this book, she also spoke with or exchanged emails with many experts in the field, including psychologists and victim's advocates. She has completed extensive training in assisting survivors and volunteers for a crisis hotline that serves victims of sexual assault.